SRA

Reading Mastery

Signature Edition

Language Arts Textbook

Siegfried Engelmann
Jerry Silbert
Susan Hanner

SRA

Columbus, OH

SRAonline.com

SRA

Printed in the United States of America.

Send all inquiries to this address:
SRA/McGraw-Hill
4400 Easton Commons
Columbus, OH 43219

ISBN: 978-0-07-612608-8
MHID: 0-07-612608-0

2 3 4 5 6 7 8 9 10 QWD 13 12 11 10 09 08 07

The McGraw-Hill Companies

Write a paragraph that reports on what happened.
Write a sentence for each name shown in the pictures.

ground	climbed	flew	jumped
landed	broke	trunk	branch

Check 1
Does each sentence tell the main thing? (M)

Check 2
Does each sentence begin with a capital and end with a period? (CP)

Check 3
Does each sentence tell what somebody or something **did?** (DID)

Write a paragraph that reports on what happened.
Write a sentence for each name shown in the pictures.

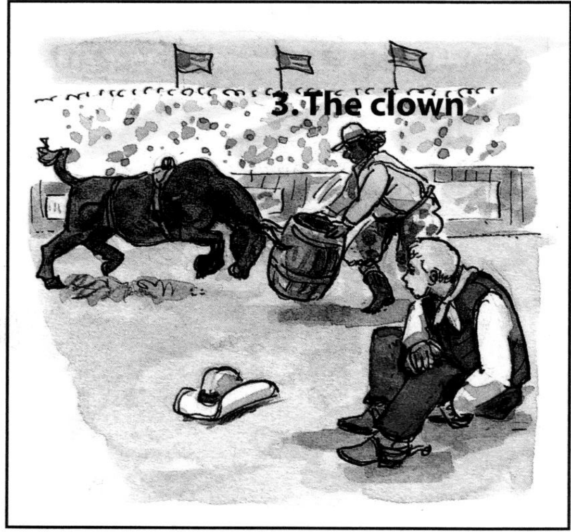

fell	ground	charged	ran	toward	barrel
hit	knocked	air	helped	walk	away

Check 1
Does each sentence tell the main thing? (M)

Check 2
Does each sentence begin with a capital and end with a period? (CP)

Check 3
Does each sentence tell what somebody or something **did?** (DID)

Write a paragraph that reports on what happened.
Write a sentence for each name shown in the pictures.

missed   Robert's head   threw   held   smelled   their

Check 1
Does each sentence tell the main thing? (M)

Check 2
Does each sentence begin with a capital and end with a period? (CP)

Check 3
Does each sentence tell what somebody or something **did?** (DID)

Write a paragraph that reports on what happened.
Write a sentence for each name shown in the pictures.

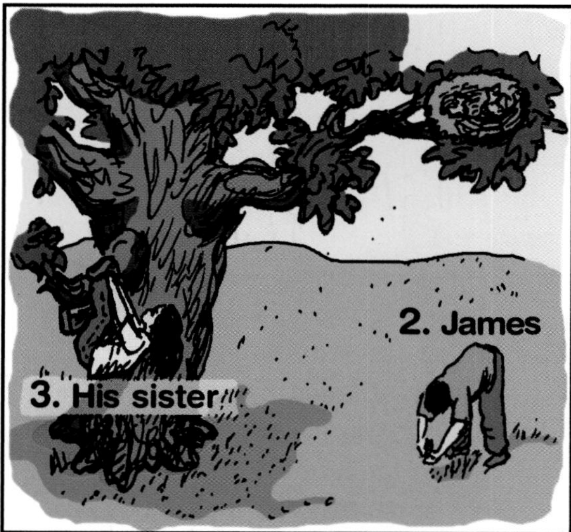

bird helped fell its nest ground climbed tree branch

Check 1
Does each sentence tell the main thing? (M)

Check 2
Does each sentence begin with a capital and end with a period? (CP)

Check 3
Does each sentence tell what somebody or something **did?** (DID)

D

Write a paragraph that reports on what happened.
Write a sentence for each name shown in the pictures.

grabbed window sill started yelled
ate piece pie answered phone scolded

Check 1
Does each sentence tell the main thing? (M)

Check 2
Does each sentence begin with a capital and end with a period? (CP)

Check 3
Does each sentence tell what somebody or something **did?** (DID)

Write a paragraph that reports on what happened.

barrel	rolled	truck	crashed
an apple	teacher	boy	caught

Check 1
Did you give a clear picture of what happened? (WH)

Check 2
Did you fix up any run-on sentences? (RO)

Check 3
Does each sentence begin with a capital and end with a period? (CP)

Check 4
Does each sentence tell what somebody or something did? (DID)

C

D

Write the verb for each sentence.

1. The boys rode their bikes.
2. Her mother was singing to herself.
3. I slipped on the ice.
4. She was eating in her room.
5. They sat on a bench.
6 My brother and sister played in the park.

Write a paragraph that reports on what happened.

gorilla walked bananas trail cage
picked escaped followed zookeeper

Check 1
Did you give a clear picture of what happened? (WH)

Check 2
Did you fix up any run-on sentences? (RO)

Check 3
Does each sentence begin with a capital and end with a period? (CP)

Check 4
Does each sentence tell what somebody or something did? (DID)

C

D

Write the verb for each sentence.

1. A happy baby was playing with her rattle.
2. Don's truck stopped at the railroad tracks.
3. They were talking to the police officer.
4. Six horses ate the long grass.
5. Bill and Tom were sleeping in the grass.
6. He felt sick.

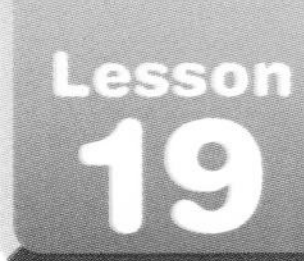

Write the verb for each sentence.

1. A young man fell off his bike.
2. Ann and her sister whispered to each other.
3. They were eating lunch.
4. The frog was sitting on the log.
5. A car and a truck stopped at the red light.
6. Six boys were sleeping on the floor.

Write sentences with words that have an apostrophe.

1. Two butterflies landed on a ______.

2. The paint dripped onto ______.

3. A mouse sat on ______.

3. A boy sat on ______.

shoe knee head shirt

Write a paragraph that reports on what happened.

Frisbee	bushes	bark	appeared
grabbed	threw	field	Alex's dog

Check 1
Did you give a clear picture of what happened? (WH)

Check 2
Did you fix up any run-on sentences? (RO)

Check 3
Does each sentence begin with a capital and end with a period? (CP)

Check 4
Does each sentence tell what somebody or something did? (DID)

C

1. The ball went between ______.

2. Two birds stood on ______.

3. The monkey pulled ______.

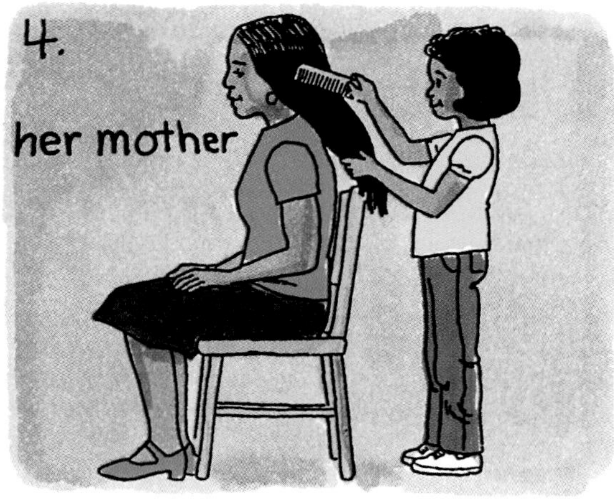

4. A girl combed ______.

hair arm tail legs

Write a paragraph that tells about the middle picture.

truck ramp tusks spare tire wheel

Check 1
Did you write sentences that give a clear picture of what must have happened in the middle picture? (WH)

Check 2
Are all your sentences written correctly? (CP, RO, DID)

Write the verb for each sentence.

1. They sat on a couch.
2. My sister and her friend were talking on the phone.
3. He walked into the room.
4. The airplane was making lots of noise.
5. A cat and a dog were in the room.
6. My older brother had a cold.

Write a paragraph that tells about the middle picture.

climbed	growled	against	bush	missed

Check 1
Did you write sentences that give a clear picture of what must have happened in the middle picture? (WH)

Check 2
Are all your sentences written correctly? (CP, RO, DID)

Rule: Words that tell what somebody or something did are verbs.

Write the five words that are verbs.

drank	played
fat	car
silly	gave
sat	boy
pretty	kicked

1.
I like to play in the grass.
Ann

2.
This popcorn is salty.
POP CORN
Kenny

3.
I can make you laugh.
A clown

1. the boys goed to Bills house. (3)
2. Alice fell asleep she was very tired. (2)
3. that boys shirt has six red buttons and four yellow buttons (3)
4. My best friends are jerry gomez and alex jordan. (4)
5. Melissa and richard put their dog on richards bed. (3)
6. We looked outside and The rain had just stopped. (2)

D

Write a paragraph that tells about the middle picture.

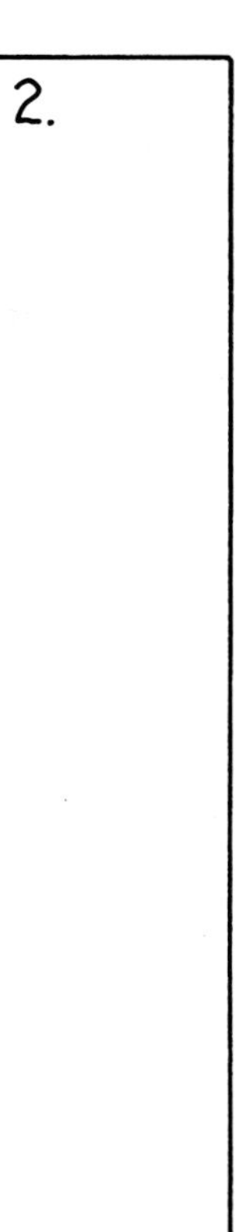

banana **climbed** **flew** **unfastened** **chain**

Check 1
Did you write sentences that give a clear picture of what must have happened in the middle picture? (WH)

Check 2
Are all your sentences written correctly? (CP, RO, DID)

1. My dad's cat had four kittens. (2)
2. She ~~teached~~ taught ~~robert~~ Robert and ~~jerry~~ Jerry how to ride a bike. (3)
3. ~~she~~ She washed the windows of her dad's car. (3)
4. We ~~seen~~ saw ~~mrs.~~ Mrs. ~~jordan~~ Jordan in the store. ~~she~~ She waved to us. (5)

Write complete sentences that tell what the people in the pictures said.

Write the verb for each sentence.

1. A red pencil fell off the table.
2. He is sitting next to the window.
3. A red car and a blue car went down the street.
4. It stopped.
5. His arms and legs were moving very quickly.
6. She has a dollar.

Write complete sentences that tell what the people in the pictures said.

Write a paragraph that tells about the middle picture.

toward galloped crashed charged fence

Check 1
Did you write sentences that give a clear picture of what must have happened in the middle picture? (WH)

Check 2
Are all your sentences written correctly? (CP, RO, DID)

Write the part of speech for each number.
Write **verb** or **pronoun.**

<u>They</u> <u>went</u> with us.
1 2

<u>He</u> went with us.
3

<u>She</u> <u>hid</u> inside the barn.
4 5

She <u>was looking</u> at <u>it</u>.
6 7

Write each sentence with the correct punctuation.
Make sure you follow these punctuation rules:

a. Put a comma after the word **said**.
b. Capitalize the first word the person said.
c. Put a period after the last word the person said.
d. Put quote marks around the exact words the person said.

1. The girl said it is time to eat
2. Mary said your dog has a sore leg
3. My brother said you look sick

Write the part of speech for each number.
Write **verb** or **pronoun.**

They were looking at her.
1 2 3

The wolf jumped out of the bushes.
4

It was very soft.
5 6

She went with him.
7 8

Write each sentence with the correct punctuation.
Make sure you follow these punctuation rules:

a. Put a comma after the word **said.**
b. Capitalize the first word the person said.
c. Put a period after the last word the person said.
d. Put quote marks around the exact words the person said.

1. His mother said what do you want
2. He said are you feeling better
3. Jim said these shoes are too big
4. She said where is the car

Write a paragraph that tells about the middle picture.

chased dove broke ground stream

Check 1
Did you write sentences that give a clear picture of what must have happened in the middle picture? (WH)

Check 2
Are all your sentences written correctly? (CP, RO, DID)

Write a short paragraph about this picture.

	Each person caught three fish.

Write a paragraph that tells about the middle picture.

boat hook fishing line pole laughed bait

Check 1
Did you write sentences that give a clear picture of what must have happened in the middle picture? (WH)

Check 2
Are all your sentences written correctly? (CP, RO, DID)

Lesson 32

B

1. Tom said, "why did you do that?" (2)
2. They seen fred and jerry at the store. (3)
3. Maria said, "i love math." (2)
4. Lisa teached Marys brother to swim. (2)
5. My sister went to the doctor and she had a cold. (3)

C

Write a short paragraph about this picture.

Carmen
I told you not to play in the mud.

Carmen gave her dog a bath.

Write the part of speech for each number.
Write **verb** or **pronoun.**

The silver wolf jumped out of the bushes.
1

It was very soft.
2

She was with him.
3 4 5

They were looking at her.
6 7 8

Write the noun in each subject.

1. A big dog chased a cat.
2. Girls played outside my house.
3. My best friend was sick.
4. That movie ended early.
5. James fell asleep.

Write a paragraph that tells about the middle picture.

climbed threw ladder apple brought

Check 1
Did you write sentences that give a clear picture of what must have happened in the middle picture? (WH)

Check 2
Are all your sentences written correctly? (CP, RO, DID)

1. They said we are hungry. (4)
2. She teached jerry to cook. (2)
3. I said are you tired? (3)
4. The bus went up the hill it made lots of noise. (2)
5. Jeff made dinner and he made a pie for dessert (4)

Write the part of speech for each number.
Write **verb** or **pronoun.**

A big wind <u>knocked</u> <u>him</u> down.
1 2

<u>He</u> <u>saw</u> <u>them</u>.
3 4 5

Bill <u>was eating</u> lunch.
6

Write the noun in each subject.

1. That yellow shirt cost ten dollars.
2. Cats are great pets.
3. His dream was to be a football player.
4. Mary was sick.
5. The old table was made of wood.

Lesson
35

C

- Our dog barked when the man walked by.
- When the man walked by, our dog barked.

Rules: Start with a capital letter.
Write the part that tells when.
Make a comma and write the rest of the sentence.
End the sentence with a period.

1. They went swimming in the morning.
2. We talked softly while the baby slept.
3. The cook took a nap after lunch.

D

Rule: If a person said more than one sentence, write everything the person said inside the quote marks.

His mother
We need some milk. Will you go to the store?

His mother said, "We need some milk. Will you go to the store?"

1.
Doug
Can I go outside? It is snowing.

2.
We went to the zoo. The monkeys made us laugh.
Abby

Write a paragraph that tells about the middle picture.

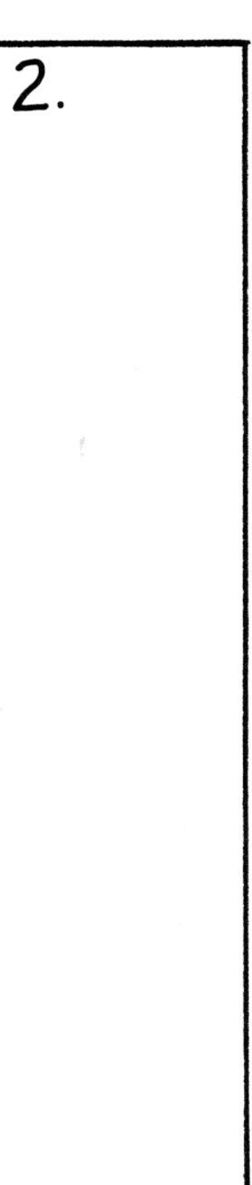

asleep | unlocked | opened | cage | key

Check 1
Did you write sentences that give a clear picture of what must have happened in the middle picture? (WH)

Check 2
Are all your sentences written correctly? (CP, RO, DID)

1.
I live in Texas. Where do you live?
James
2.
My brother will meet us. He will bring the boat.
Sally

Rewrite each sentence so it begins with the part of the predicate that tells when.

1. They cleaned the kitchen while Jane went shopping.
2. He read a book in the morning.
3. The sun came out after the rain stopped.
4. She tripped as she walked into the room.

1. James said, "Today is my birthday. We are having a party." (2)
2. Bill met Alice in the park. She said, "You look good." (4)
3. Ann's dad is very tall. He plays basketball. (3)
4. The doctor said, "You have a bad cold. Don't go outside." (4)
5. I ~~seen~~ saw Ann and Jane at Mr. Jordan's house. (5)

Write the part of speech for each number.

- Write **verb** or **pronoun.**

<u>He</u> <u>found</u> <u>it</u> on the beach.
1 2 3

<u>She</u> <u>was</u> with <u>them</u>.
4 5 6

<u>They</u> <u>were</u> above the clouds.
7 8

Rewrite each sentence so it begins with the part of the predicate that tells when.

1. She sang a song as she walked to school.
2. Jerry woke up when the bell rang.
3. A big wind blew during the night.
4. The bears slept all winter long.
5. She was tired before suppertime.

Write a paragraph that tells about the middle picture.

ice barricade icy water broke skate

Check 1

Did you write sentences that give a clear picture of what must have happened in the middle picture? (WH)

Check 2

Are all your sentences written correctly? (CP, RO, DID)

1. He said I can't find my dog. Have you seen him? (3)
2. She can drive a car and her brother taught her to drive. (3)
3. Linda adams and chris jordan were in my class (4)
4. James said, "where is Tom's shirt? He wants it back." (3)
5. My brother was sick he had a bad cold. (2)

Rewrite each sentence so it begins with the part that tells when.

1. Birds sang when the sun came up.
2. Everybody laughed as Tim walked into the room.
3. He went to sleep after he brushed his teeth.
4. They ate lunch after fixing the fence.

fed the dog

walked down the stairs

talked to the mail carrier

got into her car

Write a paragraph that tells about the middle picture.

paint	knock	through	squirt	hose

Check 1
Did you write sentences that give a clear picture of what must have happened in the middle picture? (WH)

Check 2
Are all your sentences written correctly? (CP, RO, DID)

TEST 4

Write a paragraph that tells about the middle picture.

climbed growled against bush missed swing

Check 1
Did you write sentences that give a clear picture of what must have happened in the middle picture? (WH)

Check 2
Are all your sentences written correctly? (CP, RO, DID)

Write a paragraph that tells about the first picture and the missing picture.

2.

trailer row pole boat alarm clock

	Carlos and Henry decided
	to go fishing on Saturday.

Check 1
Did you give a clear picture of what happened in the first picture? (WH)

Check 2
Did you give a clear picture of what must have happened in the middle picture? (WH)

Check 3
Are all your sentences written correctly? (CP, RO, DID)

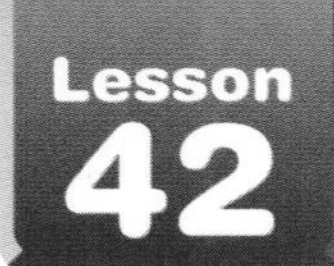

For each picture, write a sentence that begins with a part that tells when.

2.

Bill ate lunch.

Bill went outside.

1 *o'clock*

Write a paragraph that tells about the first picture and the missing picture.

2.

tied	through	skate	horse	paws

Sandra decided to take her dog ice skating at the pond.

Check 1
Did you give a clear picture of what happened in the first picture? (WH)

Check 2
Did you give a clear picture of what must have happened in the middle picture? (WH)

Check 3
Are all your sentences written correctly? (CP, RO, DID)

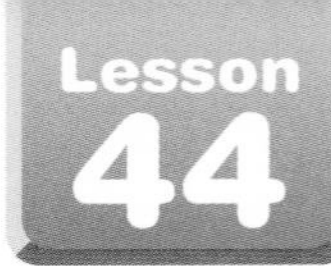

1. At midnight, The dog began to bark. (2)
2. The streets flooded, during the rainstorm. (2)
3. She bought a book, Before the store closed. (2)
4. While the wind blew, Everybody stayed inside Toms house.
5. Ann fell asleep while toms dad sang. (2)
6. Two old trees fell down, last night. (1)
7. Before Anns dad made breakfast we washed our hands. (2)

1. When alice got to school, Nobody was there. (3)
2. Jerry asked his mother, can I stay home?" (3)
3. Tom asked his sister, where is my shirt (5)
4. My sister wasn't home. She went to alices house. (2)
5. As mr. jordan left, The children waved to him. (4)
6. Bill cleaned his room, before he ate breakfast (2)

C

brushed his teeth

combed his hair

washed his face

D Write a paragraph that tells about the first picture and the missing picture.

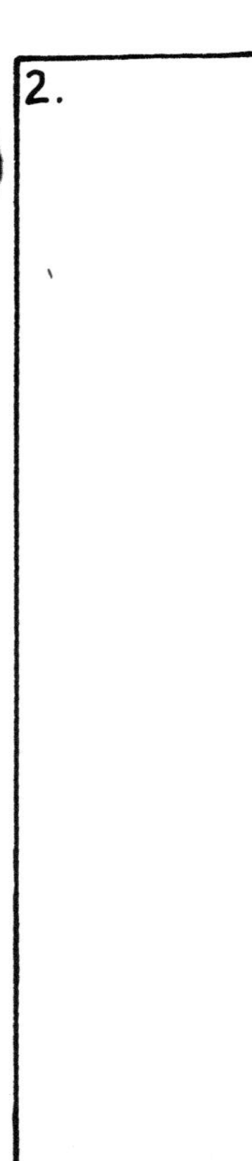

emptied	kitchen	garbage	apron
wastebasket	sandwich	mopped	groceries

Jerry's friends had a big lunch at Jerry's house.

Check 1
Did you give a clear picture of what happened in the first picture? (WH)

Check 2
Did you correctly punctuate the sentence that tells what somebody said? (Q)

Check 3
Did you give a clear picture of what must have happened in the middle picture? (WH)

Check 4
Are all your sentences written correctly? (CP, RO, DID)

Here are short parts that tell when: **at last, suddenly, next, now.**
All these parts tell when. If you write one of these parts at the beginning of the sentence, put a comma after it.

1. Rita saved money for a year. __________, she had enough money to buy a bike.
2. First, Tom got a paint brush. __________, he got a can of paint.
3. The car was going down the street. __________, it made a great noise and stopped.
4. Tina put on her hat and coat. __________, she was ready to go outside.

Write a paragraph that tells about the first picture and the missing picture.

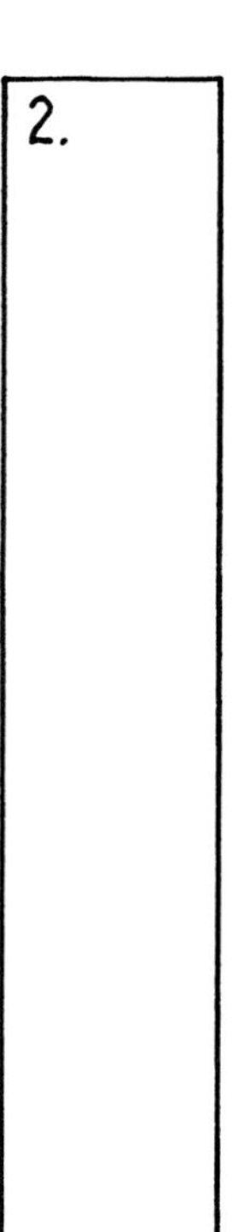

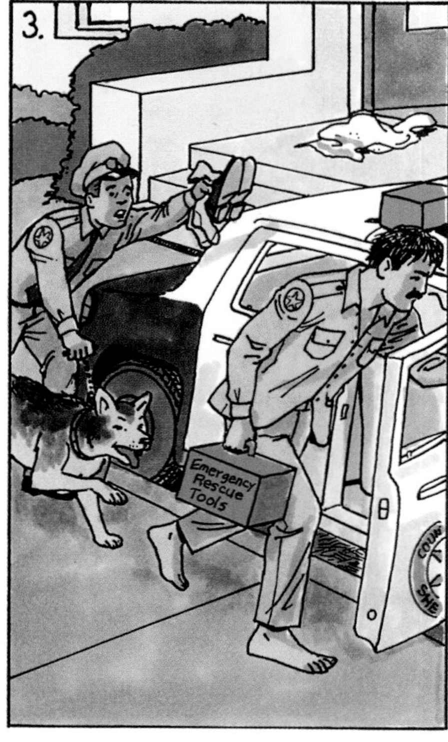

towel · leash · shoes · shower · carried · police dog · open · dried · grabbed

The sheriff took a shower at the end of a hard day of work.

Check 1
Did you give a clear picture of what happened in the first picture? (WH)

Check 2
Did you correctly punctuate the sentence that tells what somebody said? (Q)

Check 3
Did you give a clear picture of what must have happened in the middle picture? (WH)

Check 4
Are all your sentences written correctly? (CP, RO, DID)

B

1. Bill asked his mother, when will we eat dinner (5)
2. When the dog barked at a cat, The baby woke up. (2)
3. Tom brushed his teeth, after he washed his face (2)
4. Abdul said, "I am hungry. I want an apple (2)
5. The boys cleaned their teachers desk. (1)
6. Where is mr. suzuki (3)

Write the letters of all the houses each description could tell about.

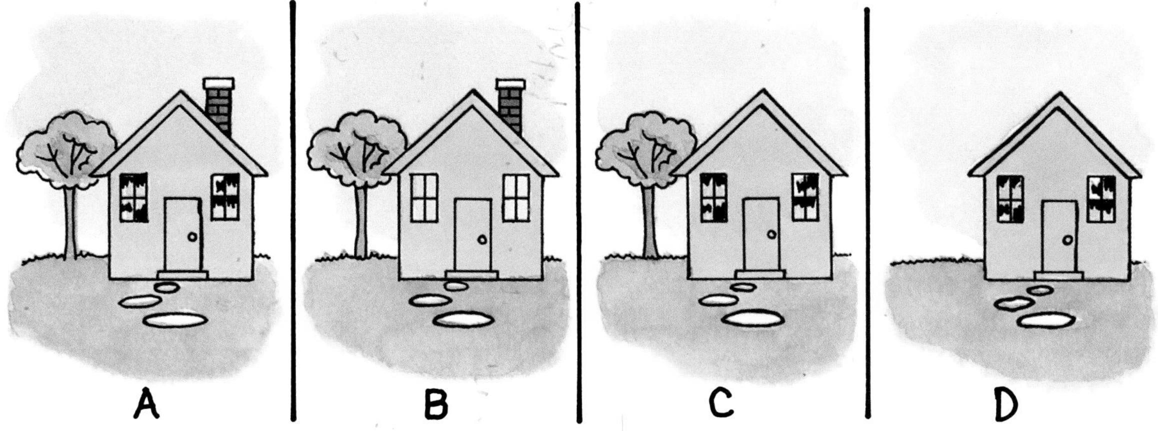

1. The house had broken windows. It had a front door.
2. The house had broken windows. It had a chimney.
3. The house had broken windows. It had a tree next to it.

Write a paragraph that tells about the first picture and the missing picture.

paint	almost	rail	clothes	brushes	bucket

Jill was almost finished painting the porch rail.

Check 1
Did you give a clear picture of what happened in the first picture? (WH)

Check 2
Did you correctly punctuate the sentence that tells what somebody said? (Q)

Check 3
Did you give a clear picture of what must have happened in the middle picture? (WH)

Check 4
Are all your sentences written correctly? (CP, RO, DID)

Mary flew her kite in the morning. A great wind came up suddenly. Mary's kite went high into the clouds. That kite was in the air for three hours.

Write the letters of all the kites each description could tell about.

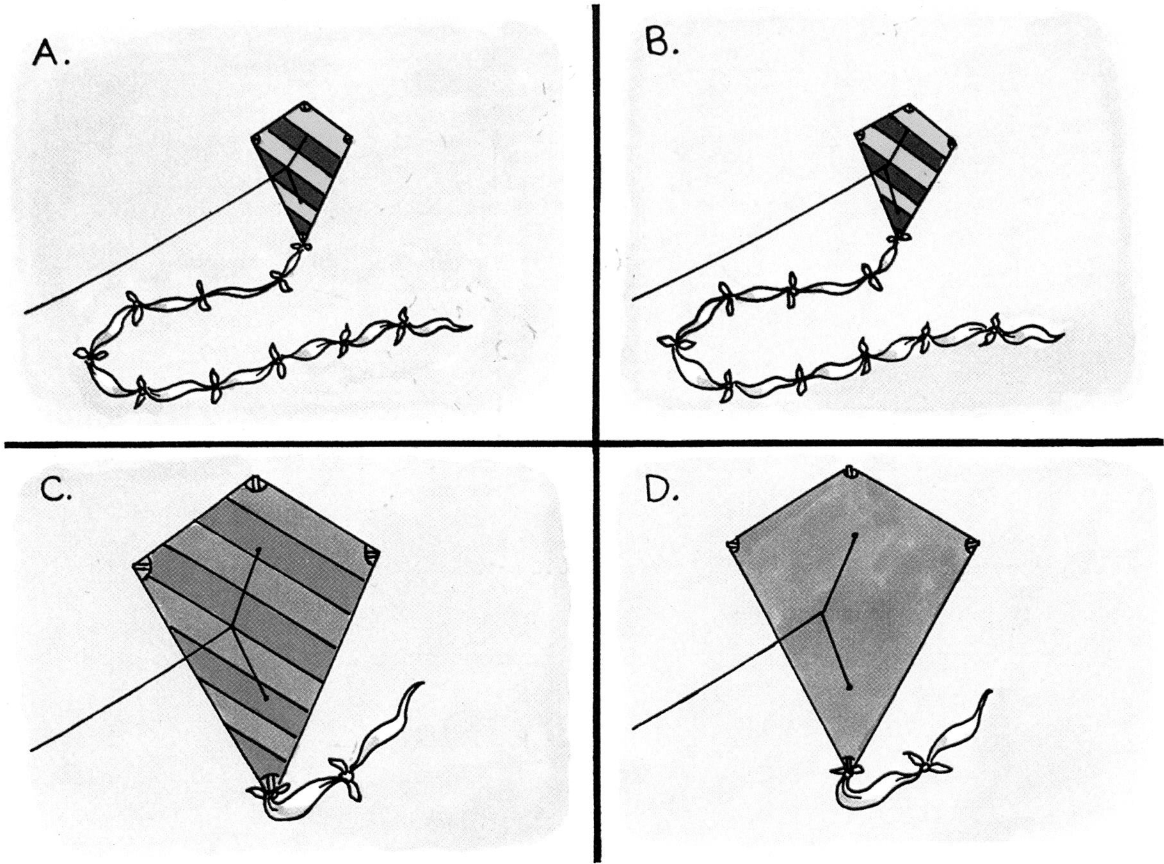

1. The kite had stripes. The kite also had a long tail.
2. The kite was big. The kite had a short tail.
3. The kite had a short tail. The kite also had stripes.

Write a description that has two sentences.

- First, write a sentence that tells about house A, house C or house D. Begin that sentence with the words **the house**.
- Next, write a sentence so that your whole description tells only about house A. Begin that sentence with the words **the house.**

A

B

C

D

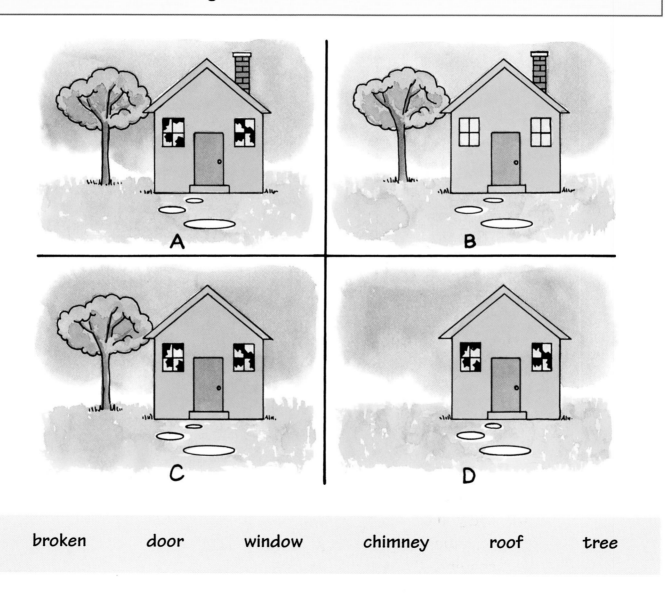

broken door window chimney roof tree

Write a paragraph that tells about the first picture and the missing picture.

2.

chain wheel tools twist puzzled o'clock

The back wheel of Alicia's bike was badly bent.

Check 1
Did you give a clear picture of what happened in the first picture? (WH)

Check 2
Did you correctly punctuate the sentence that tells what somebody said? (Q)

Check 3
Did you give a clear picture of what must have happened in the middle picture? (WH)

Check 4
Are all your sentences written correctly? (CP, RO, DID)

Write a description that has two sentences.

- First, write a sentence that tells about hat B, hat C or hat D.
- Next, write a sentence that makes your description tell only about hat B. Start your description with the words **the hat.**

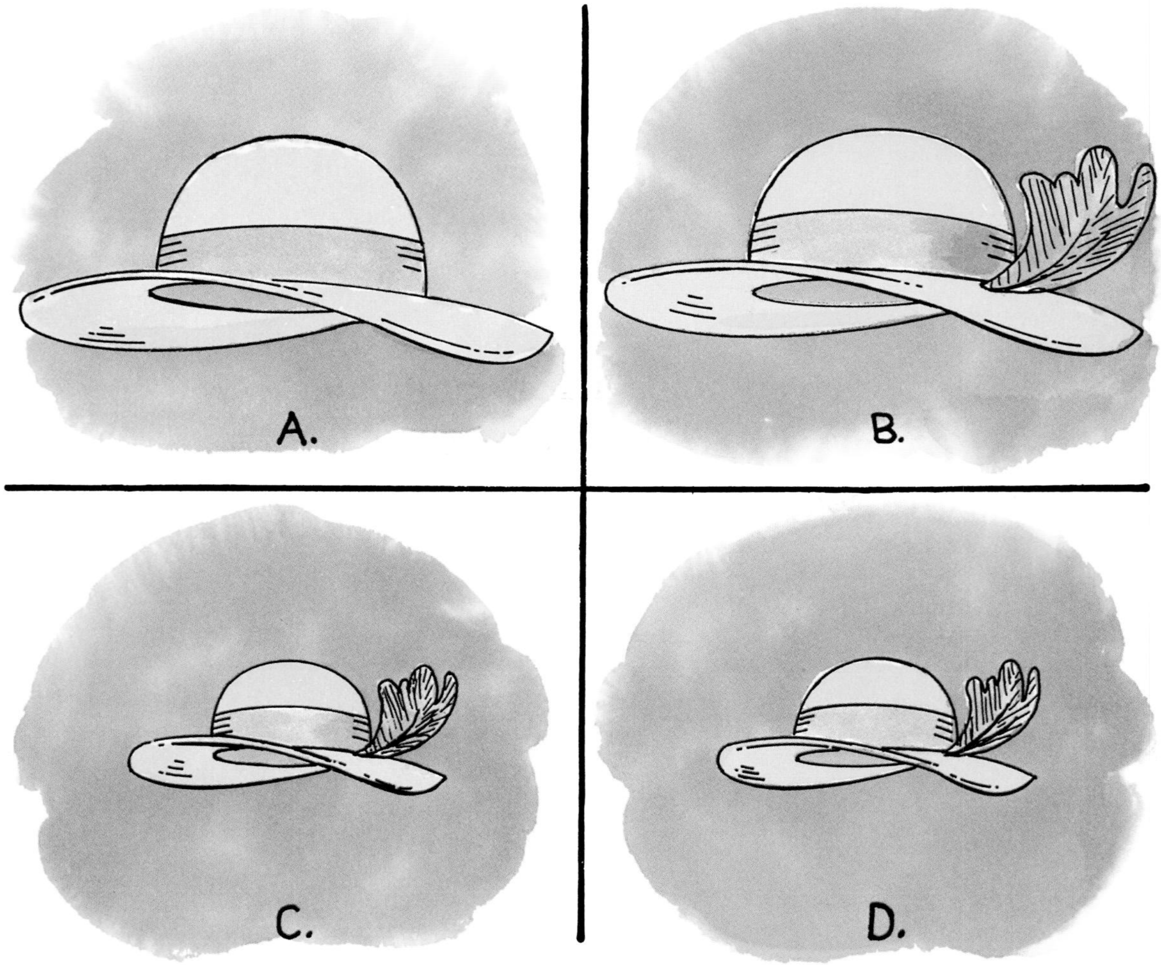

A.

B.

C.

D.

feather small large

1. Alice asked, "where is my car (3)
2. After mr. adams ate he went home. (3)
3. James asked his mother can I go out to play?" (3)
4. Alice sat down, when she finished the race. (1)
5. Two birds flew over anns head (3)

Rewrite each sentence so the word **and** appears only once.

1. My mother and my father and my brother were sleeping.
2. We ate cereal and eggs and pancakes for breakfast.
3. I bought an apple and an orange and a peach.

1. Write a description about picture 1. Tell where the girls were and what they were doing.

2. Write a description about picture 2. Tell where the girls were and what they were doing.

Write a paragraph that tells about the first picture and the missing picture.

clothesline dried clothes climb water campsite blanket

When the bridge broke, Tom fell into the stream.

Check 1
Did you give a clear picture of what happened in the first picture? (WH)

Check 2
Did you correctly punctuate the sentence that tells what somebody said? (Q)

Check 3
Did you give a clear picture of what must have happened in the middle picture? (WH)

Check 4
Are all your sentences written correctly? (CP, RO, DID)

Lesson 55

Rules about nouns:

Some nouns are always capitalized no matter where they appear in sentences.

A person's name is always capitalized.

Days of the week are always capitalized.

Months of the year are always capitalized.

1. January
2. Tuesday
3. Sunday
4. September
5. Carlos

For each noun, write **day, month** or **name.**

1. Bill Lee
2. Thursday
3. December
4. February
5. Saturday
6. James

sandals chair bathing suit hammer table nails

1. Make up a sentence that tells the things the man painted.
2. Make up a sentence that tells what the woman wore.
3. Make up a sentence that tells the things the man carried.

Write a paragraph that tells about the first picture and the missing picture.

2.

tractor engine attach

	Ted was repairing a fence when he
	heard a car making funny noises.

Check 1
Did you give a clear picture of what happened in the first picture? (WH)

Check 2
Did you correctly punctuate the sentence that tells what somebody said? (Q)

Check 3
Did you give a clear picture of what must have happened in the middle picture? (WH)

Check 4
Are all your sentences written correctly? (CP, RO, DID)

1. Write a sentence that tells the things Rosa did.

hung up the phone put on her coat went outside

2. Write a sentence that tells the things Jason did.

Write a paragraph that tells about the first picture and the missing picture.

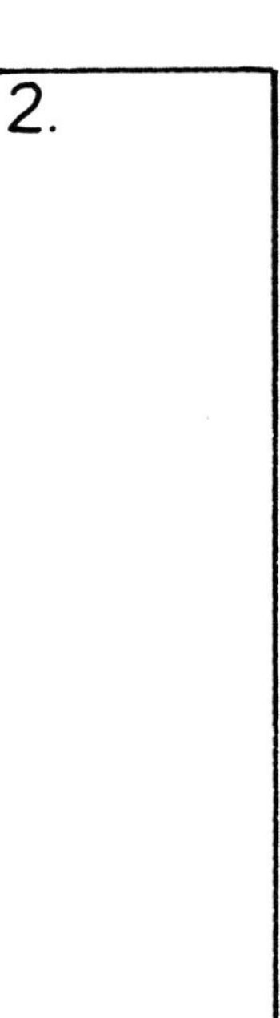

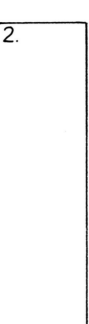

ax	carried	built	toolbox
chopped	dragged	sign	shelter

	Ron's boat sank near a desert
	island.

Check 1
Did you give a clear picture of what happened in the first picture? (WH)

Check 2
Did you correctly punctuate the sentence that tells what somebody said? (Q)

Check 3
Did you give a clear picture of what must have happened in the middle picture? (WH)

Check 4
Are all your sentences written correctly? (CP, RO, DID)

1. Tom and I was both born on the first wednesday in december. (3)

2. Janes hand got dirty when she planted trees (3)

3. Ann visited her grandmother every monday night in april and may. (3)

4. Cats and dogs was running in Toms yard. (2)

5. Alex and i were talking to cora. (2)

6. Kay asked her dad can i stay up late? (5)

7. When mr. adams got home on Thursday. He read the newspaper. (4)

Write a sentence that tells the things **a janitor** did.

chalkboard | chair | wash | swept

B

1. Mr. Adams and mrs. sanchez was sick on wednesday. (4)

2. Jill asked Tom can i help you?" (4)

3. When my mom walked into the room My baby sister smiled. (2)

4. Where did you put Jills coat (2)

5. You was born in february. (2)

6. She asked was he born in september or october?" (5)

Write a sentence that tells the things that **Ann and Sue** did.

TEST 6

Write a paragraph that tells about the first picture and the missing picture.

bear   elephant's trunk   cage   climbed   fence   lifted

	Bob talked to the zookeeper while
	his sister Leslie leaned against the
	fence and looked at the bears.

Check 1
Did you give a clear picture of what happened in the first picture? (WH)

Check 2
Did you correctly punctuate the sentence that tells what somebody said? (Q)

Check 3
Did you give a clear picture of what must have happened in the middle picture? (WH)

Check 4
Are all your sentences written correctly? (CP, RO, DID)

Write two paragraphs.

- Write one paragraph that tells about the first picture.
- Write one paragraph that tells about the missing picture and the last picture.

beach ocean bike change

clothes suit uniform swimming

Check 1

Does your first paragraph give a clear picture of what happened in the first picture? (WH)

Check 2

Does your second paragraph give a clear picture of what happened in the middle picture and the last picture? (WH, P)

Check 3

Are all your sentences written correctly? (CP, RO, DID, Q)

Sentences that have a noun in the subject may have **adjectives** in the subject. Words that come before the noun are adjectives. These words tell about the noun. They tell **what kind** or **how many.**

Here are adjectives that tell **what kind:**

old dog **small** dog **mean** dog **nice** dog

Here are adjectives that tell **how many:**

a dog **one** dog **each** dog **some** dogs

1. These red apples taste great.
2. My older brother is sick.
3. The pennies landed on the ground.
4. Flies were buzzing around the food.

For each sentence, copy the subject.

- Write **N** above the noun.
- Write **A** above each adjective.

1. Our teacher gave books to the children.
2. A man fixed her water pipes.
3. Nine red bugs were on my sandwich.
4. My younger sister fixed our car.

Write **R** for each fact that is relevant.
Write **No** for each fact that is not relevant.

Why didn't Mary cook hamburgers?

1. She didn't have any hamburger buns.
2. Everybody in her family loved hamburgers.
3. She told everybody that she would fix hamburgers.
4. She didn't have time to go to the store and buy hamburger buns.
5. She had lots of hamburger meat.

For each sentence, copy the subject.

- Write **N** above the noun.
- Write **A** above each adjective.

1. Seven little bugs were on the table.
2. Her best friend was not in school.
3. Dogs chased the cats.
4. An airplane landed on the runway.
5. Their mother played the piano.
6. His blue pants are too tight.

Write the letters of the sentences that are **not** relevant to the question.

Why are doors important?

(a) Doors keep the cold out of houses in the winter. (b) Heaters are also important for keeping houses warm. (c) Doors keep flies out of the house in the summer. (d) Some doors have fancy doorknobs. (e) Some doors can keep fires from spreading from one room to another room.

Write two paragraphs.

- Write one paragraph that tells about the first picture.
- Write one paragraph that tells about the missing picture and the last picture.

2.

igloo	crashed	crawl	covered	built
snowmobile	saw	frozen	lake	women

Check 1
Does your first paragraph give a clear picture of what happened before the first picture and in the first picture? (WH)

Check 2
Does your second paragraph give a clear picture of what happened in the middle picture and the last picture? (WH, P)

Check 3
Are all your sentences written correctly? (CP, RO, DID, Q)

1. Jerry asked, "can Raymond and i go to the movies" (4)
2. My dads hand is twice as big as Jerrys hand. (2)
3. When the baby fell asleep Everybody was happy. (2)
4. Alice Chuck and ellen ate lunch at Ellens house. (3)
5. December january and february was cold months. (4)
6. Alice was very tired, when she got home on monday. (2)

Write the letters of the sentences that are **not** relevant to the question.

Why do people like dogs?

(a) Dogs can be good friends to people. (b) Some people like cats. (c) Dogs can make a house very dirty. (d) Dogs protect little children. (e) Dogs guard a house when nobody is home. (f) Some dogs run into the street to chase cars. (g) Dogs are fun to play with.

Write two paragraphs.

- Write one paragraph that tells about the first picture.
- Write one paragraph that tells about the missing picture and the last picture.

tires — too tall — air — stopped — tunnel
their truck — drove — couldn't — through

Check 1
Does your first paragraph give a clear picture of what happened before the first picture and in the first picture? (WH)

Check 2
Does your second paragraph give a clear picture of what happened in the missing picture and the last picture? (WH, P)

Check 3
Are all your sentences written correctly? (CP, RO, DID, Q)

Write two paragraphs.

- Write one paragraph that tells about the first picture.
- Write one paragraph that tells about the missing picture and the last picture.

2.

trailer	row	pole	boat	alarm clock	middle

Check 1
Does your first paragraph give a clear picture of what happened before the first picture and in the first picture? (WH)

Check 2
Does your second paragraph give a clear picture of what happened in the middle picture and the last picture? (WH, P)

Check 3
Did you write at least two sentences that begin with a part that tells when? (W, COM)

Write two paragraphs.

- Write one paragraph that tells about the first picture.
- Write one paragraph that tells about the missing picture and the last picture.

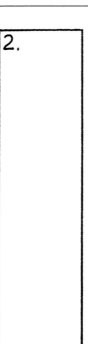

unlock ate climb sneak banana
jungle sleep snore key

Check 1
Does your first paragraph give a clear picture of what happened before the first picture and in the first picture? (WH)

Check 2
Does your second paragraph give a clear picture of what happened in the missing picture and the last picture? (WH, P)

Check 3
Did you write at least two sentences that begin with a part that tells when? (W, COM)

Write two paragraphs.

- Write one paragraph that tells about the first picture.
- Write one paragraph that tells about the missing picture and the last picture.

emptied kitchen garbage
wastebasket sandwich mopped groceries

Check 1
Does your first paragraph give a clear picture of what happened before the first picture and in the first picture? (WH)

Check 2
Does your second paragraph give a clear picture of what happened in the missing picture and the last picture? (WH, P)

Check 3
Did you write at least two sentences that begin with a part that tells when? (W, COM)

Lesson 72

1. When the bell rang, we went to our classroom.
   (A N P V A N)
2. Linda stood in front of a large desk.
   (N V A A N)
3. That tiny black fly flew into my cup.
   (A A A N V A N)
4. During the night, a strong wind blew.
   (A N A A N V)

1. They will be sad if they lose the game.
2. He will go with us unless he is sick.
3. She won the race although she had a bad cold.

1. During the big storm, we went inside an old house.
2. He saw many black ants on the kitchen table.
3. Two old men helped her.
4. His truck moved slowly up a steep hill.
5. After the meeting, she went to the store.

Instructions: Write each sentence so it begins with the part that can be moved.

1. We will be very happy if we win the game.
2. She will win the race unless she falls down.
3. The field was dry although it rained all night.

D

Here's a rule about using verbs when you write a story: When you start a story, you can write sentences that tell where somebody **was,** or what somebody **was doing.** After you tell where somebody was or what somebody was doing, you tell what the person **did,** **not** what the person was doing.

suddenly tripped watch edge grabbed coat

Check 1
Do your sentences about picture 1 tell what Mrs. Hart **was doing** and what her dog **was doing?** (WH)

Check 2
Do your sentences for the other pictures tell what Mrs. Hart **did** and what her dog **did?** (WH, DID)

Check 3
Do you have two sentences for each picture—one sentence for Mrs. Hart and one sentence for her dog? (WH)

1. I found four red marbles under that old rug.
2. Every day, we buy milk at the store.
3. An airplane flew over a big white cloud.
4. A bright light came from the third floor.

1. The mississippi river is the longest river in the united states. (4)
2. Texas alaska and california are the biggest states. (3)
3. Is los angeles bigger than san francisco? (4)
4. We lived on baldwin street until last september. (3)
5. After she brushed her teeth, She went to bed. (2)
6. My favorite cities are new york dallas and miami. (5)
7. Ann asked mr. james Where can i buy that book (7)

Instructions: Write each sentence so it begins with the part that can be moved.

1. She went to the show although she was not feeling well.
2. We will go swimming unless it rains.
3. He will get sick if he keeps on eating so much.

A N P V A N A N
1. After the storm, we had a fish in our basement.

A N V P A A N
2. His mother told us a funny story.

A N A N V V P
3. In my dream, five tigers were chasing me.

N N V A N
4. Tom and Fran ran over that hill.

1. When we got home, the dog started howling.
2. The air was cold in the morning.
3. After he ate lunch, he took a nap.
4. He painted a picture as he talked on the phone.

D Write a paragraph that reports on what happened.

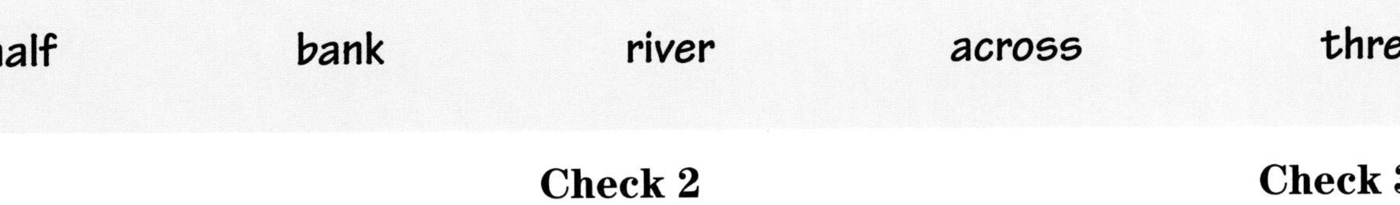

Check 1
Do your sentences about picture 1 tell where Sam and Ann **were** and what they **were doing?** (WH)

Check 2
Do your sentences for the other pictures tell what Sam **did** and what Ann **did?** (WH, DID)

Check 3
Do you have at least 2 sentences for each picture? (WH)

N N V A N
1. Fran and Ray ran to the beach.

A N P V A N A A N
2. In the evening, I saw big spiders on our front steps.

A A N V A A N
3. That old car runs like a new car.

P V A A N
4. He slipped on the icy stairs.

1. When the car started, the lights came on.
2. We watched football on Monday night.
3. After she fixed the car, she made dinner.
4. He fell asleep while he was watching TV.
5. She brushed her teeth before she went to sleep.

D

1.

sheriff

deputy

2.

That bridge doesn't seem safe.

3.

4.

point   broke   bridge   behind

Check 1

Do your sentences about picture 1 tell where the sheriff and his deputy **were** and what they **were doing?** (WH)

Check 2

Do your sentences for the other pictures tell what somebody or something **did?** (WH, DID)

Check 3

Do you have at least one sentence that begins with a part that tells when? (W, COM)

1. The empire state building is in new york. (5)
2. Robert fed the dog washed the dishes and cleaned his room before lunch. (1)
3. Is mexico larger than canada (3)
4. Jill asked, "Where is Dr. Lees office? (2)
5. I bought apples oranges and pears at the store. (1)
6. December january and february are the coldest months of the year. (3)
7. Yokos sister lives on washington street. (3)
8. Tom and his sister was in the park. (1)

Instructions: Move the part that tells when and rewrite each sentence.

1. In the morning, we went to the park.
2. He ran home after the rain stopped.
3. She put on a hat as she walked out the door.
4. On Saturday, we stayed at home.
5. When they came home from school, they milked the cows.

A A A N V P
1. A large red truck stopped in front of them.

N A N A N V A N
2. After school, six boys and two girls played in the gym.

P V P V A A N A A N
3. She helped him fix the flat tire on his new bike.

Instructions: Rewrite all the sentences so that the part that tells when is moved.

1. Everybody was happy by the end of the day.
2. We finished our work before we went outside.
3. As they walked home, they talked about the movie.
4. When he woke up, he felt sick.

D

cage stump climb swept snore rope asleep swinging

Check 1
Do your sentences about picture 1 tell where Fred and the monkey **were** and what they **were doing?** (WH)

Check 2
Do your sentences for the other pictures tell what Fred **did** and what the monkey **did?** (WH, DID)

Check 3
Do you have at least one sentence that begins with a part that tells when? (W, COM)

Write a passage that has two paragraphs.

couch   alarm clock   o'clock   paw   ear

Check 1
Does your first paragraph tell where the characters were and what each character was doing? (WH)

Check 2
Does your second paragraph tell what the alarm clock did and what the characters did? (DID, WH)

Check 3
Did you write at least one sentence that begins with a part that tells when? (W, COM)

Rules for writing a good story:

- Start by telling where the characters were and what they were doing.
- Then tell what they did. Make sure you tell about all the things that happened so your story gives a clear picture.

Write a passage that has two paragraphs.

tail huge newspaper buggy basketball
scare suddenly toward wagged

Check 1
Does your first paragraph tell where the characters were and what each character was doing? (WH)

Check 2
Does your second paragraph tell what the dog did and what the characters did? (DID, WH)

Check 3
Did you write at least one sentence that begins with a part that tells when? (W, COM)

Use the table of contents in Reading Textbook B to answer these questions.

1. What's the lesson number for the selection that begins on page 121?
2. What's the title of the selection that begins on page 121?
3. What's the lesson number for the selection that begins on page 191?
4. What's the title of the selection that begins on page 191?

Write the address for each item.

1. Orlando Florida

2. Street number: 485
   Street name: Lake Avenue
   City name: Detroit
   State name: Michigan

3. Street number: 22
   Street name: Hidden Valley Road
   City name: Cleveland
   State name: Ohio

Use the words below to make an alphabetical list.

only *monkey* *happen* *baby* *answer* *don't*

Some word parts are called prefixes. Prefixes are the first part of some words. Some prefixes have a clear meaning.

Words	Opposites
1. agree	
2. appear	
3. like	
4. honest	

1.
Ginger
Fred
2.
What happened?

Write a story that has three paragraphs.

motorboat facing crash wade shore trailer toward

Check 1
Does your first paragraph tell where the characters were and what each character was doing? (WH)

Check 2
Do your other two paragraphs tell what happened in pictures 2, 3, 4 and 5? (WH, DID)

Check 3
Did you write at least two sentences that begin with a part that tells when? (W, COM)

1.
Skateboard Contest
Tom
Lisa
A small dog
Skateboard Contest

2.
I'm going to get first prize.

Write a story that has three paragraphs.

between ramp high awarded sensational

Check 1
Does your first paragraph tell where the characters were and what each character was doing? (WH)

Check 2
Do your other two paragraphs tell what happened in pictures 2, 3 and 4? (WH, DID)

Check 3
Did you write at least two sentences that begin with a part that tells when? (W, COM)

Use the words below to make an alphabetical list.

label	decide	captain
enormous	middle	forever

Write the word for each description.

1. What word means **the opposite of appear?**
2. What word means **to start again?**
3. What word means **not clean?**
4. What word means **not fair?**
5. What word means **the opposite of like?**
6. What word means **not aware?**

Use the table of contents in Reading Textbook B to answer these questions.

1. What's the lesson number for the selection that begins on page 137?
2. What's the title of the selection that begins on page 137?
3. What's the lesson number for the selection that begins on page 323?
4. What's the title of the selection that begins on page 323?

1. What word means **without effort?**
2. What word means **without a home?**
3. What word means **the opposite of connect?**
4. What word means **to connect again?**
5. What word means **not zipped?**
6. What word means **without a hat?**

1.
Sid
Mary
Alice
2.
Where's Alice?

Write a story that has three paragraphs.

rodeo staircase arena program
row barrel through grabbed

Check 1
Does your first paragraph tell where the characters were and what each character was doing? (WH)

Check 2
Do your other two paragraphs tell what happened in pictures 2, 3, 4 and 5? (WH, DID)

Check 3
Did you write at least two sentences that begin with a part that tells when? (W, COM)

Lesson 90—Test 9

1. Write the date for the tenth day of August in the year 1886.

Write the address with commas.

1. Street number: 305
2. Street name: Market Street
3. City name: Salem
4. State name: Oregon

Use the table of contents in Reading Textbook B to answer these questions.

1. What's the lesson number for the selection that begins on page 110?
2. What's the title of the selection that begins on page 110?

Write the word for each description.

1. What word means **the opposite of approve?**
2. What word means **not happy?**
3. What word means **to write again?**

Use the table of contents in your Reading Textbook B to answer these questions.

1. What's the lesson number for the selection that begins on page 335?
2. What's the title of the selection that begins on page 335?
3. What's the lesson number for the selection that begins on page 53?
4. What's the title of the selection that begins on page 53?

Write the word for each description.

1. What word means **without trees?**
2. What word means **without form?**
3. What word means **to approve again?**
4. What word means **the opposite of approve?**
5. What word means **without joints?**
6. What word means **without clouds?**

Write the words in alphabetical order.

oven
once
officer
ocean
outfit

Rule: You can have only one person talk in a paragraph. When another person talks, you must have that person talk in the next paragraph.

Write a passage that tells what happened.

2.

balloon float above parade watch
bought because tied crowd

Check 1
Does each paragraph have no more than one person talking?

Check 2
Does your first paragraph tell where the characters were and tell about the problem they had?

Check 3
Do the rest of your paragraphs give a clear picture of what the characters said and did?

Write the first page in your Reading Textbook B that tells about each topic.

1. leopard
2. wheel dogs
3. nerves
4. air tank
5. galaxy

Write the words in alphabetical order.

boast
building
blew
breath
beyond
billows

Write the word for each description.

1. What word means **full of harm?**
2. What word means **the opposite of pleased?**
3. What word means **without a voice?**
4. What word means **to light again?**
5. What word means **without joy?**
6. What word means **full of joy?**

D Write a passage that tells what happened.

touch | display case | brontosaur

Check 1
Does each paragraph have no more than one person talking?

Check 2
Does your first paragraph tell where the characters were and what they were doing?

Check 3
Do the rest of your paragraphs give a clear picture of what the characters said and did?

Lesson 94

Write the word for each description.

1. What word means **being hard?**
2. What word means **being tender?**
3. What word means **the opposite of belief?**
4. What word means **full of thought?**
5. What word means **without thought?**
6. What word means **being bright?**
7. What word means **not happy?**
8. What word means **without a point?**

Write the word for each description.

1. What word means **to write again?**
2. What word means **being fair?**
3. What word means **the opposite of agree?**
4. What word means **not finished?**
5. What word means **without hope?**
6. What word means **being fresh?**
7. What word means **being close?**
8. What word means **without a coat?**

Write a passage that tells what happened.

window shoulders groceries sitting reach burn smoke

Check 1
Does each paragraph have no more than one person talking?

Check 2
Does your first paragraph tell where the characters were and what they were doing?

Check 3
Do the rest of your paragraphs give a clear picture of what the characters said and did?

Lesson 96

Write the word for each description.

1. What word means **one who rides?**
2. What word means **being sad?**
3. What word means **full of thought?**
4. What word means **the opposite of approve?**
5. What word means **one who runs?**
6. What word means **without joy?**
7. What word means **being dull?**
8. What word means **not done?**
9. What word means **without sleeves?**
10. What word means **to build again?**

Lesson 97

Write the word for each description.

1. What word means **to type again?**
2. What word means **being mean?**
3. What word means **to wash again?**
4. What word means **one who washes?**
5. What word means **one who bakes?**
6. What word means **without taste?**
7. What word means **full of skill?**
8. What word means **being round?**
9. What word means **without care?**
10. What word means **one who tastes?**

Write an interesting ending to the story your teacher read. Your ending should have at least three paragraphs.

money operation hundred enough decide
sidewalk because wallet thousand

Barbara took the wallet and went to ______.

Check 1
Does each paragraph have no more than one person talking?

Check 2
Did you write at least two sentences that begin with a part that tells when?

Write the word for each description.

1. What word means **being hard?**
2. What word means **very hard?**
3. What word means **being cold?**
4. What word means **very cold?**
5. What word means **the opposite of colored?**
6. What word means **to color again?**
7. What word means **full of tears?**
8. What word means **without tears?**
9. What word means **being bright?**
10. What word means **very bright?**
11. What word means **not healthy?**

Use Reading Textbook B to answer these questions.

1. What part of the textbook gives an alphabetical listing of topics that appear in the book?
2. On what page does the topic **porpoise** first appear in the textbook?
3. Write the first word on that page.
4. What's the last page on which the topic **porpoise** appears?
5. Write the last word on that page.

Write the word for each description.

1. What word means **one who sits?**
2. What word means **being narrow?**
3. What word means **without pain?**
4. What word means **being firm?**
5. What word means **very firm?**
6. What word means **not firm?**
7. What word means **one who gives?**
8. What word means **to give again?**
9. What word means **without water?**
10. What word means **one who speaks?**

Use Reading Textbook B to answer these questions.

1. What part of the textbook gives an alphabetical listing of topics that appear in the book?
2. On what page does the topic **galaxy** first appear in the textbook?
3. Write the first word on that page.
4. What's the last page on which the topic **galaxy** appears?
5. Write the last word on that page.

Write an interesting ending to the story your teacher read. Your ending should have at least four paragraphs.

treasure   chest   pirate   shovel   suddenly

Check 1
Does each paragraph have no more than one person talking?

Check 2
Did you write at least two sentences that begin with a part that tells when?

Lesson 100—Test 10

Write a passage that tells what happened.

kitchen surprise groceries space creature blanket shoulders

Check 1
Does each paragraph have no more than one person talking?

Check 2
Does your first paragraph start out by telling where Sally was and what she was doing?

Check 3
Do the rest of your paragraphs give a clear picture of what the characters said and did?

Here's how to write interesting stories:

1. **Tell about the characters at the beginning of the story.**
   Tell where they were.
   Describe them and name them.
2. **Tell about their problem.**
   Tell what they wanted to do and why they couldn't do it.
3. **Tell the things they did to solve their problem.**
4. **Tell how the story ends.**
   Tell whether they solved their problem.

Write an interesting story.

embarrassed   money   wallet   suddenly   blushed   glared

These are questions about the story you wrote. If the answer to all nine questions is **yes,** you wrote a super story. If any answer is **no,** you'll fix up the story so the answer is **yes.** Then you'll have a super story.

Questions about the problem.

1. Did you give the man a name?
2. Did you describe the man?
3. Did you tell where he was and what he did before he discovered that he had a problem?
4. Did you tell what the man's problem was?
5. Did you tell where he was when he discovered that he had a problem?
6. Did you tell how he felt when he discovered that he had a problem?

Questions about the rest of the story.

7. Did you tell some things the man said to the woman?
8. Did you tell some things the woman said to the man?
9. Did you tell what the man did after the woman agreed to a plan?

Check 1
Does your story answer all nine questions?

Check 2
Did you write at least three sentences that begin with a part that tells when?

Check 3
Are all your sentences punctuated correctly?

Write the word for each description.

1. What word means **one who plays?**
2. What word means **to play again?**
3. What word means **can be played?**
4. What word means **can be washed?**
5. What word means **one who washes?**
6. What word means **not washed?**
7. What word means **being light?**
8. What word means **the opposite of agree?**
9. What word means **can be managed?**

Write an interesting story.

vacation	factory	beach	island
enjoyed	horseback	wonderful	decided

containers games holidays

Write these words in alphabetical order.

banana	electric	special	amaze	decide
plastic	people	early	hundred	purple

C

Write the word for each description.

1. What word means **can be read?**
2. What word means **not read?**
3. What word means **without hair?**
4. What word means **full of pain?**
5. What word means **the opposite of honest?**
6. What word means **can be believed?**
7. What word means **can be touched?**
8. What word means **to watch again?**

These are questions about the story you wrote. If the answer to all eight questions is **yes,** you wrote a super story. If any answer is **no,** you'll fix up the story so the answer is **yes.** Then you'll have a super story.

Questions about the problem.

1. Did you give the women names?
2. Did you tell where they were and what they were doing?
3. Did you tell about their problem?
4. Did you tell why they hadn't done what they dreamed about?

Questions about the rest of the story.

5. Did you tell how the women got the money they needed?
6. Did you tell whether they took a vacation or quit their jobs?
7. Did you tell where they went and what they did?
8. Did you tell how they felt at the end of your story?

Check 1
Does your story answer all eight questions?

Check 2
Did you write at least three sentences that begin with a part that tells when?

Check 3
Are all your sentences punctuated correctly?

Write the word for each description.

1. What word means **can be washed?**
2. What word means **to count wrong?**
3. What word means **without stars?**
4. What word means **not seen?**
5. What word means **to label again?**
6. What word means **to label wrong?**
7. What word means **can be walked?**
8. What word means **being tough?**
9. What word means **to name wrong?**

Write an interesting story.

spaceship creature frightened suddenly

Write these words in alphabetical order.

count	collar	complete	cob
cod	coat	cone	cook

1.
2.
3.
4.
5.
6.
7.
8.

Write the word for each description.

1. What word means **being gentle?**
2. What word means **to understand wrong?**
3. What word means **full of joy?**
4. What word means **to read wrong?**
5. What word means **can be moved?**
6. What word means **without fear?**
7. What word means **one who paints?**
8. What word means **not cooked?**
9. What word means **to place wrong?**

These are questions about the story you wrote. If the answer to all five questions is **yes,** you wrote a super story. If any answer is **no,** you'll fix up the story so the answer is **yes.** Then you'll have a super story.

Questions about the problem.

1. Did you name the woman and her dog?
2. Did you tell where they were and what they were doing when they discovered that they had a problem?
3. Did you describe the problem?
4. Did you tell what the space creature wanted?
5. Did you tell all the things that happened after the picture?

Check 1
Does your story answer all five questions?

Check 2
Did you write at least three sentences that begin with a part that tells when?

Check 3
Are all your sentences punctuated correctly?

Write these words in alphabetical order.

dry driver draft dream drop drum

1.
2.
3.
4.
5.
6.

Write the word for each description.

1. What word means **to lead wrong?**
2. What word means **being strange?**
3. What word means **in a strange way?**
4. What word means **in a quiet way?**
5. What word means **not finished?**
6. What word means **the opposite of approve?**
7. What word means **full of care?**
8. What word means **in a sweet way?**
9. What word means **without sun?**

C

mountains crawled edge front cliff tire

tumbled narrow roof suddenly

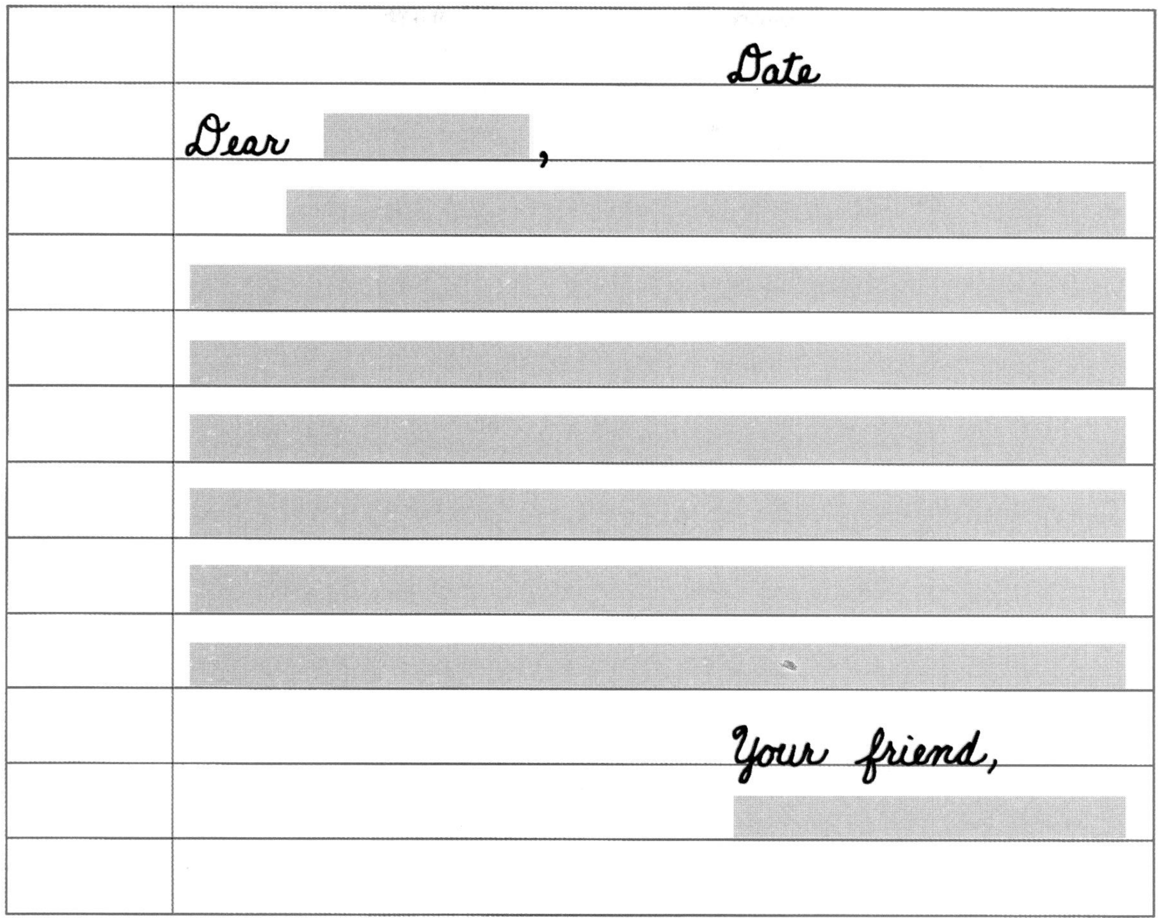

Check 1
Did you write the date and the name of the person you're writing?

Check 2
Did you sign the letter?

Check 3
Did you tell all the things that happened?

Lesson 108

cents		cops
	can	
	certain	
	cup	
	chip	
	circus	
	clipper	
	call	
	city	

Write the word for each description.

1. What word means **in a rough way?**
2. What word means **being rough?**
3. What word means **to clean again?**
4. What word means **one that cleans?**
5. What word means **without hope?**
6. What word means **in a complete way?**
7. What word means **to do wrong?**
8. What word means **in a kind way?**
9. What word means **can be read?**

chief		clean
	circle	
	chill	
	chew	
	chirp	
	copy	
	chin	
	chunk	
	class	
	claw	

Write the word for each description.

1. What word means **to do again?**
2. What word means **being quiet?**
3. What word means **very brave?**
4. What word means **not real?**
5. What word means **without worth?**
6. What word means **one who follows?**
7. What word means **not told?**
8. What word means **being calm?**

C

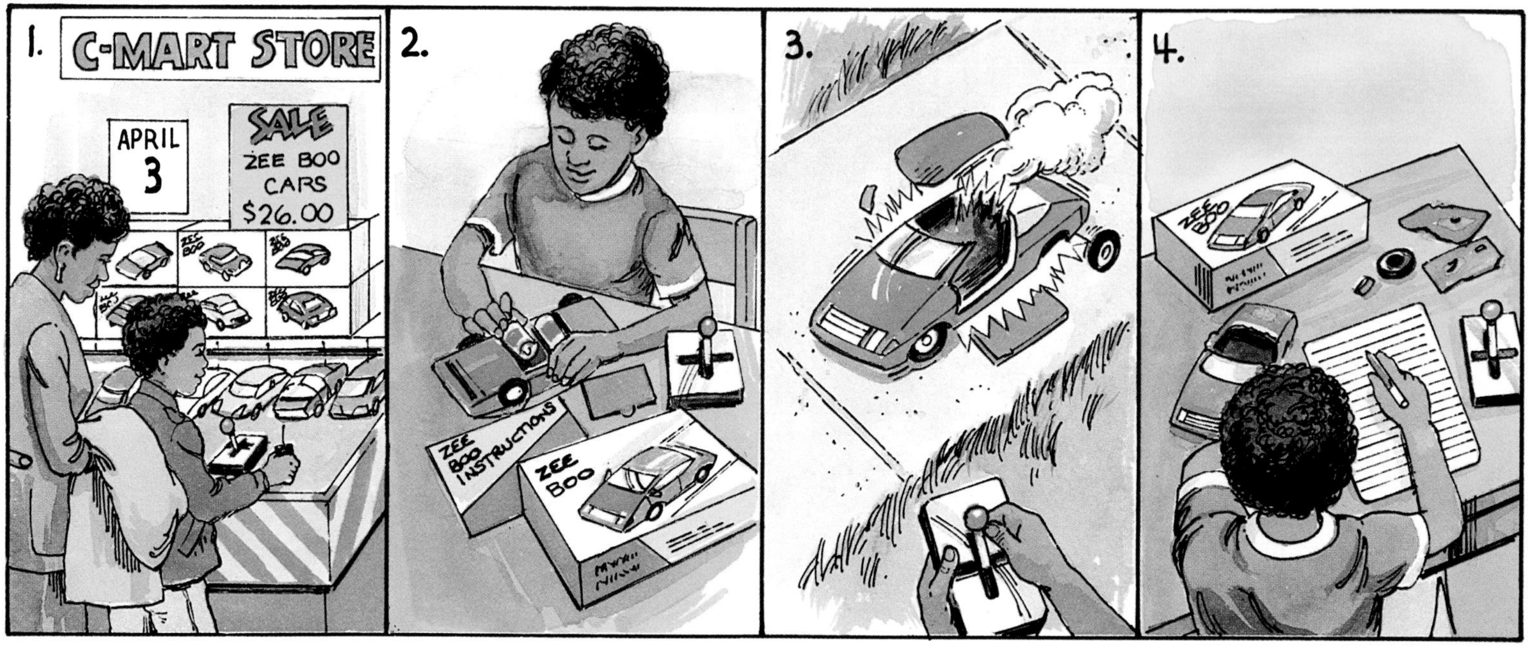

1.
2.
3.
4.

directions suddenly pieces batteries
exploded instructions followed

Write a letter to the Zee Boo Car Company.

- Write everything you need on top.
- Copy the first sentence. Then write the rest of the letter. Tell what happened. Then tell what you want the company to do about it.

Your address
City, State ZIP Code
April 3, 20__

Mr. Z. Y. Zee
Zee Boo Car Company
1000 Boo Street
Flint, Michigan 48501

Dear Mr. Zee:

I am sending you the pieces of a Zee Boo Car.

Sincerely,
Your full name

Lesson 110—Test 11

Write these words in alphabetical order.

twice	raccoon	track
really	turtle	rose

Write the word for each description.

1. What word means **being bright?**
2. What word means **one who drives?**
3. What word means **without trees?**
4. What word means **very bright?**
5. What word means **in a sad way?**
6. What word means **can be washed?**
7. What word means **full of care?**
8. What word means **to spell wrong?**

For each sentence, write the word the goes in the blank.

1. The dog and the cat ______ to sleep in the sun. (like, likes)
2. My mother ______ very carefully. (drive, drives)
3. The birds ______ in the morning. (sing, sings)
4. She ______ very well. (write, writes)
5. They ______ a new car. (need, needs)

Lesson 110

Pretend that you are an inventor. You have taken your invention to an invention fair. It's in a box that's labeled **Top Secret. Write a paragraph about your invention.** Tell what the invention does and why it's top secret.

1. Did you write everything you need on top?
2. Did you tell where you bought the car and how much you paid for it?
3. Did you tell about following the instructions carefully?
4. Did you tell what happened when you took the car outside?
5. Did you tell that you want your money back?
6. Did you write **Sincerely,** and your full name at the end of the letter?

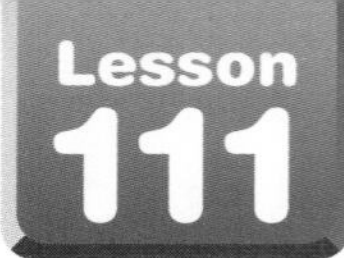

Pretend that you are an astronaut on a space shuttle that is about to blast off into the sky. Write 3 sentences that describe how you would feel and what you might be thinking. Start each sentence with **I.**

Use the glossary in Reading Textbook B to answer the questions.

1. What are the guide words for the word **insist?**
2. What are the guide words for the word **reef?**

Write the word for each description.

1. What word means **without wings?**
2. What word means **one who skates?**
3. What word means **not written?**
4. What word means **without roads?**
5. What word means **to cut again?**
6. What word means **not planned?**
7. What word means **being rude?**
8. What word means **one who listens?**

Zee Boo Car Company
1000 Boo Street
Flint, Michigan 48501

April 11, 20...

Your name
Your address
City, State ZIP Code

Dear (your name):

We are returning the pieces of your Zee Boo car. We are sorry but we cannot refund your money. The car was on sale. Its regular price is $37.95, but C-Mart sold it for $26.00. When cars are on sale, we do not guarantee them. You may contact C-Mart to see if they will refund your money.

Sincerely,

X. Y. Zee

X. Y. Zee

Lesson 111

E

Facts that may help you write a good letter.

- You have the receipt that shows you paid 26 dollars for the Zee Boo car.
- Your mother has shopped at C-Mart for the last 15 years.
- Your mother spends more than 300 dollars a year at C-Mart.

F

Your address
City, State ZIP Code
April 14, 20___

Ms. Nancy Sloan
C-Mart
2400 Market Lane
Flint, Michigan 48507

Dear Ms. Sloan

I bought a Zee Boo Car at C-Mart on April 3.

Sincerely,
Your full name

refund   instructions   exploded   pieces

Make sure your letter answers all these questions.

- Did you tell where you bought the Zee Boo car and when you bought it?
- Did you tell what you did with the Zee Boo car and what happened to the car?
- Did you tell about your letter to the Zee Boo Car Company?
- Did you tell what the Zee Boo Car Company told you in their letter?
- Did you tell C-Mart what you want them to do?
- Did you tell what your mother will do if they don't refund your money?

Guide Words

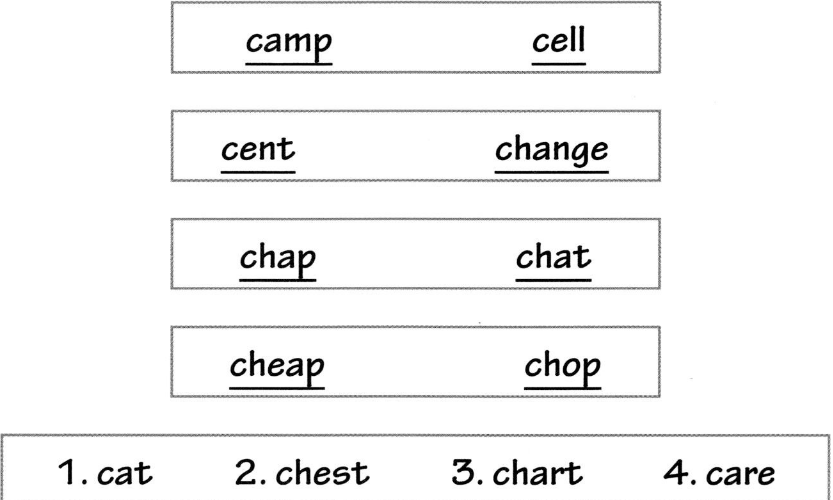

camp cell
cent change
chap chat
cheap chop
1. cat 2. chest 3. chart 4. care

Write the word for each description.

1. What word means **not cut?**
2. What word means **without smoke?**
3. What word means **one who leads?**
4. What word means **the opposite of allow?**
5. What word means **not lit?**
6. What word means **being slow?**

C–Mart
2400 Market Lane
Flint, Michigan 48507

April 20, 20...

Your name
Your address
City, State ZIP Code

Dear (your name):

We thank you for your letter. We are very sorry that your Zee Boo Car did not operate properly. We are also sorry for any inconvenience that you may have had.

We cannot refund your money and we understand that you do not want another Zee Boo car. The enclosed package contains two Zee Boo cars. If either one of them does not operate properly, please return it to us and we will replace it with another Zee Boo car or a different car of your choice.

Thank you for shopping at C-Mart.

Sincerely,

Nancy R. Sloan

Nancy R. Sloan

Pretend that you own a pet shop and you found all the animals out of their cages. Write a paragraph that tells what you saw, how you felt and what you did.

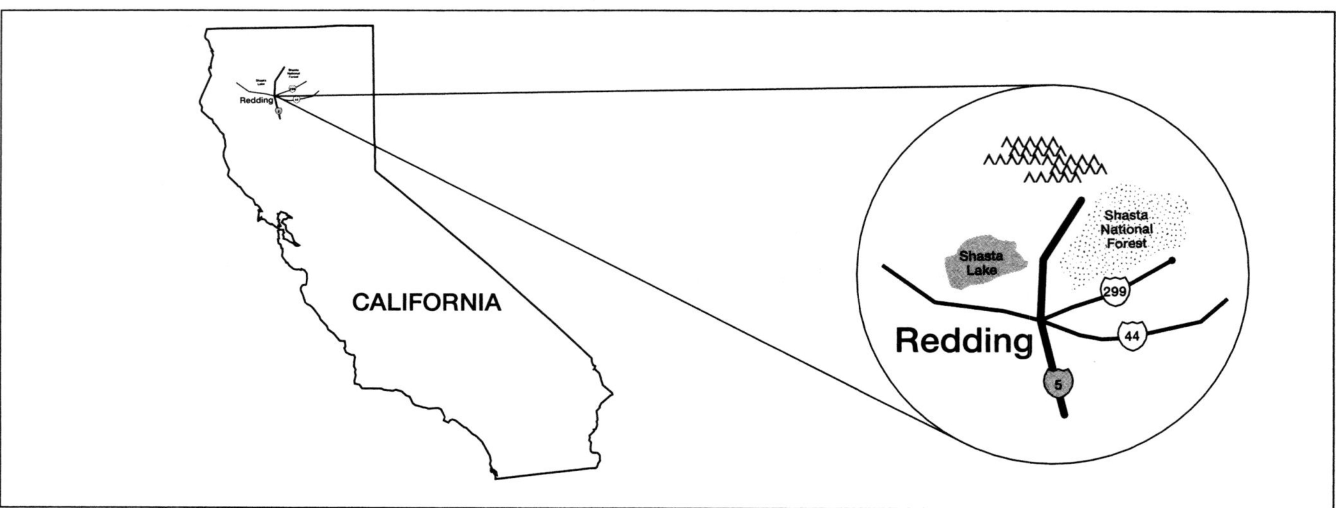

Read each item to yourself. Write **fact** or **opinion.**

1. Redding is a city in California.
2. Redding is the nicest place to live.
3. Redding is close to Shasta Lake.
4. All other cities should try to be more like Redding.
5. There are mountains to the north of Redding.
6. Redding has great weather during all times of the year.
7. If you like places where there's a lot to do, you'll love Redding.
8. The trees around Redding are the best in the world.
9. Everybody you'll meet in Redding is very friendly.

1. **descend** They will descend the hill.
   - go up
   - go down
   - eat
2. **harrow** The farmer came home with an old harrow.
   - an animal
   - a tool
   - a person
3. **lavish** Her house was very lavish.
   - small
   - clean
   - more than someone needs

Read each item to yourself. Write **fact** or **opinion.**

1. Motorcycling is more fun than anything else.
2. Motorcycles get better gas mileage than cars.
3. The best looking motorcycles are red.
4. Passengers on motorcycles are always comfortable.
5. When roads are icy or slippery, motorcycles may be dangerous.
6. Everybody who loves speed loves motorcycles.

Make a poem from this story.

STORY

There once was a king. Ring was his name.

He always carried so much gold that he looked elderly.

The gold was so heavy he couldn't stand up tall. Sometimes, he would have to crawl around.

He was a terrible sight. He called in a doctor late one evening.

The doctor said his problem was he was carrying too much gold with him. So he weighed a lot, even though he was a slim man.

So the king left his gold at home after that night. And from then on, he could stand up the right way.

Now his face is full of smiles. He can walk a long, long way.

POEM

- There once was a king
  ____
- He always carried so much gold,
  ____
- He couldn't stand up tall.
  ____
- He was a terrible sight.
  ____
- The doctor said the king had too much gold on him.
  ____
- The king left his gold at home after that night.
  ____
- Now his face is full of smiles.
  ____

Pretend that you are going to be flying on an airplane for the first time. Write a paragraph that tells about what you are thinking and how you feel.

Make an outline.

1. breakfast
   A. ____________________
   B. ____________________
   C. ____________________
   D. ____________________
2. lunch
   A. ____________________
   B. ____________________
   C. ____________________
   D. ____________________
3. dinner
   A. ____________________
   B. ____________________
   C. ____________________
   D. ____________________

1. **macaw** They saw a macaw in the jungle.
   - a large tree
   - a colorful bird
   - a kind of pond
2. **oddment** They had a lot of oddments after they finished the dinner.
   - stomach pains
   - dirty dishes
   - leftover food
3. **raiment** Their raiment was stolen.
   - luggage
   - clothing
   - animals

Make a poem from this story.

STORY

Cal was a big green duck. But Cal was not very lucky.

Things always went bad for Cal. Nobody wanted to be his friend.

When Cal was around, things were never good. They never went the way they should go.

One day, there wasn't a cloud in the sky. As soon as Cal started to fly, clouds appeared all over.

One duck said, "I'll make a bet. Before Cal lands, we'll all be covered with water."

That duck was absolutely right. Everything was flooded before the night was over.

POEM

- Cal was a big green duck.

  ____

- Things always went bad for Cal.

  ____

- When Cal was around, things were never good.

  ____

- One day, there wasn't a cloud in the sky.

  ____

- One duck said, "I'll make a bet."

  ____

- That duck was absolutely right.

  ____

Make an outline.

1. winter

2. spring

3. summer

4. fall

B

1. **sanction** The mayor sanctioned our plan.
   - approved of
   - fought
   - paid no attention to
2. **velocity** The plane had a lot of velocity.
   - fuel
   - passengers
   - speed
3. **diminutive** His daughter was quite diminutive.
   - small
   - quiet
   - pretty

Make a poem from this story.

STORY

Nearby lived a goose that the ducks learned to hate. They thought she was mean, but she thought she was good.

The ducks said to Cal, "See if you can make that goose your friend."

Cal went over to the goose and just said, "Hi." As he spoke, an eagle came out of the air.

The goose saw the eagle and flew far away. And the ducks never saw her after that time.

Cal told the others, "I couldn't make that goose my pal." Those ducks said, "But now a lot of ducks really love you, buddy."

POEM

- Nearby lived a goose that the ducks learned to hate.

  ____
- The ducks said to Cal,

  "______________________________"
- Cal went over to the goose and just said, "Hi."

  ____
- The goose saw the eagle and flew far away.

  ____
- Cal told the others, "I couldn't make that goose my pal."

  ____

When I Was Younger

1. When I was

2. When I was

3. When I was

B

Use your dictionary to find the correct meaning of the underlined word in each sentence. Write the correct meaning.

1. She did not deduct the correct amount.
   - take away
   - add
   - change
2. She collected three granules of sand.
   - bags
   - cups
   - grains

C

For each item, write the guide words for the page where you would find the word in your Reading Textbook B glossary.

Word	Guide Words	
1. familiar		
2. comment		
3. permit		

Write about a person you respect.

Why I Respect [redacted]

A person I really respect is (tell who) [redacted]. I respect [redacted] because (tell why) [redacted].

One time (tell something the person did that you respect) [redacted].

Another time (tell something else the person did that you respect) [redacted].

I hope (tell what you hope about that person) [redacted].

Use your dictionary to find the correct meaning of the underlined word in each sentence. Write the correct meaning.

1. Her grandfather had a large residence.
   - television
   - house
   - automobile
2. Sarah bought a bassoon.
   - fish
   - musical instrument
   - expensive stone

For each item, write the guide words for the page where you would find the word in Reading Textbook B glossary.

Word	Guide Words
1. success	
2. musher	
3. beware	

Write the name of the part of the book you would use for each item. The answer to each item is **glossary, index,** or **table of contents.**

1. You want to find out what selection starts on page 151.
2. You want to find out on what page the textbook first discusses baboons.
3. You want to find out what the word **billion** means.
4. You want to find out how many reading selections are presented in lesson 132.
5. You want to find out the page number for the first selection in lesson 86.
6. You want to find out the first page number for the topic **equipment.**
7. You want to find the lesson number for the selection that starts on page 93 of your textbook.

Use your dictionary to find the correct meaning of the underlined word in each sentence. Write the correct meaning.

1. She emptied the bucket of <u>cinders</u>.
   - small bits of plastic
   - clumps of dirt
   - partly burned coal
2. The <u>expense</u> for the party was too much.
   - noise
   - people invited
   - money spent

For each word, underline the prefix. Circle the root. Make a line over the suffix.

1. return
2. teacher
3. superclean
4. brightness
5. disappear

Write the name of the part of the book you would use for each item. The answer to each item is **glossary, index,** or **table of contents.**

1. You want to find out on how many pages the topic **pressure of snow** appears.
2. You want to find out the first page number for the topic **pyramid.**
3. You want to find out how many reading selections are presented in lesson 128.
4. You want to find out what the word **veld** means.
5. You want to find out the page number for the first selection in lesson 79.
6. You want to find out on what page the textbook first discusses **squid.**

Pretend that you promised to clean your room, but you forgot to do it. You hear your mother walking into the kitchen after she has been shopping. Write a paragraph. Tell how you feel. Tell what you will do.

Write about places you would like to visit.

Places I Would Like To Visit

Places I would like to visit are ______ and ______.

Here are the reasons I would like to visit ______.

One reason is ______.

Another reason is ______.

Here are the reasons I would like to visit ______.

One reason is ______.

Another reason is ______.

For each word, underline the prefix. Circle the root. Make a line over the suffix.

1. helpful
2. result
3. retain
4. contain
5. dismiss
6. unhappiness

Write the name of the part of the book you would use for each item. The answer to each item is **glossary, index,** or **table of contents.**

1. You want to find out the page number for the first selection in lesson 84.
2. You want to find out on what page the textbook first discusses **lead dogs.**
3. You want to find out the first page number for the topic **blood vessels.**
4. You want to find out what the word **plunge** means.
5. You want to find out how many reading selections are presented in lesson 124.

Use your dictionary to find the correct meaning of the underlined word in each sentence. Write the correct meaning.

1. We had <u>mullet</u> for dinner.
   - a vegetable
   - a fish
   - a fruit
2. His mother is an <u>aviator</u>.
   - pilot
   - doctor
   - nurse

Lesson 123

For each word, underline the prefix. Circle the root. Make a line over the suffix.

1. subjective
2. inject
3. detainment
4. reject
5. revert
6. inverted

Write the name of the part of the book you would use for each item. The answer to each item is **glossary, index,** or **table of contents.**

1. You want to find out on what page the textbook first discusses **stars.**
2. You want to find out what the word **exchange** means.
3. You want to find out the lesson number for the selection that starts on page 86 of your textbook.
4. You want to find out the page number for the first selection in lesson 102.
5. You want to find out on how many pages the topic **dragonflies** appears.

For each item, write the guide words for the page in the Reading Textbook B glossary on which you can find the word.

Word	Guide Words
1. dedicated	
2. weary	
3. thorough	

Write about a time you did something that you are proud of.

Something I Am Proud Of

I did something that I am proud of (tell when) ______. I was (tell where) ______. I was there because (tell why) ______.

(Tell what happened. Tell what you did that you are proud of. Tell all the important things. ______.

For each word, underline the prefix. Circle the root. Make a line over the suffix.

1. produce
2. reply
3. reduce
4. diverting

For each item, write **glossary** or **index.**

1. You want to find out on what page the textbook first discusses **lungs.**
2. You want to find out what the word **miserable** means.
3. You want to find out on how many pages the topic **moon** appears.
4. You want to find out what the word **compete** means.

Answer the questions about each simile.

- **Her teeth were like pearls.**

1. What two things are the same?
2. How were her teeth like pearls?

- **Her eyes were like diamonds.**

3. What two things are the same?
4. What's the same about her eyes and diamonds?

- **They work as hard as ants.**

5. What two things are the same?
6. What's the same about how they work and how ants work?

Answer the questions.

1. What do we call expressions that use the words **like** or **as** and that tell about things that are the same?
   - **That man moved like a turtle.**
2. What two things are the same?
3. How are they the same?
   - **The team worked like a well-designed machine.**
4. What two things are the same?
5. How are they the same?
   - **They ran like deer.**
6. What two things are the same?
7. How are they the same?
   - **Her smile was as warm as the sun.**
8. What two things are the same?
9. How are they the same?

For each word, underline the prefix. Circle the root. Make a line over the suffix.

1. mistake
2. smoothly
3. waterless
4. unhappiness
5. revisit
6. kissable

Use your dictionary to find the correct meaning of the underlined word in each sentence.

1. We could see fish in the shoals.
   - shallow water
   - dirty water
   - deep water
2. My dad planted a poplar in our yard.
   - a tree
   - a shrub
   - a flower

	My Favorite Animal
	My favorite animal is (tell what
	animal) ________.
	Here are three things I really like
	about (tell what animal):
	1. One thing I really like about (tell what
	animal) is ________.
	2. Another thing I really like about (tell
	what animal) is ________.
	3. Another thing I really like about (tell
	what animal) is ________.
	I hope (write what you hope about
	yourself and your favorite animal) ________.

Answer the questions about each metaphor.

- **Her eyes were diamonds.**

1. What two things are the same?
2. How are they the same?

- **Her teeth were pearls.**

3. What two things are the same?
4. How are they the same?

- **Her muscles were rocks.**

5. What two things are the same?
6. How are they the same?

Write the meaning for each underlined word.

1. Some of the people were very sad, but others were <u>elated</u>.
2. Her brother was very rich, but she was <u>impecunious</u>.
3. Bret's explanations were always clear, but Andy's explanations were always <u>ambiguous</u>.

- not clear
- poor
- happy

For each word, underline the prefix. Circle the root. Make a line over the suffix.

1. dishonestly
2. useful
3. misuse
4. refillable
5. recline
6. helpless
7. distress

Lesson
127

Write if each item is a simile or a metaphor.

1. Her fingers were like claws.
2. Their cat was a ghost.
3. The clouds were puffs of whipped cream.
4. His head was as bald as a basketball.
5. He had feet like paddles.

Write the meaning for each underlined word.

1. The twins were not the same. One of them was very shy. The other was very extroverted.
2. Sometimes she was very thoughtful. At other times, she was cavalier.
3. Most of the time her voice was loud. But sometimes, her voice was inaudible.
    - not thoughtful
    - not shy
    - soft

Use your dictionary to find the correct meaning of the underlined word in each sentence. Write the correct meaning.

1. The group walked toward the portal of the zoo.
    - exit
    - center
    - entrance
2. I intend to go to the movies tonight.
    - hope
    - plan
    - saved

Write if each item is a simile or a metaphor.

1. Her legs were string beans.
2. He ran like a rabbit.
3. She was dressed in a rainbow.
4. His mind worked like a computer.
5. She was as strong as a bull.
6. The cake was as light as a feather.
7. Her hair was golden straw.

Write the synonym for each underlined word.

1. The boys had some money for the movie, and the girls also had some <u>currency</u>.
2. Jan was always careful when danger was near. Her brother was not as <u>cautious</u> as she was.
3. Bret's explanations were always very short. Bret's mother also gave explanations that were <u>brief</u>.
4. Some of the workers did not mind being poor, but others complained because they were so <u>indigent</u>.

- very short
- careful
- money
- poor

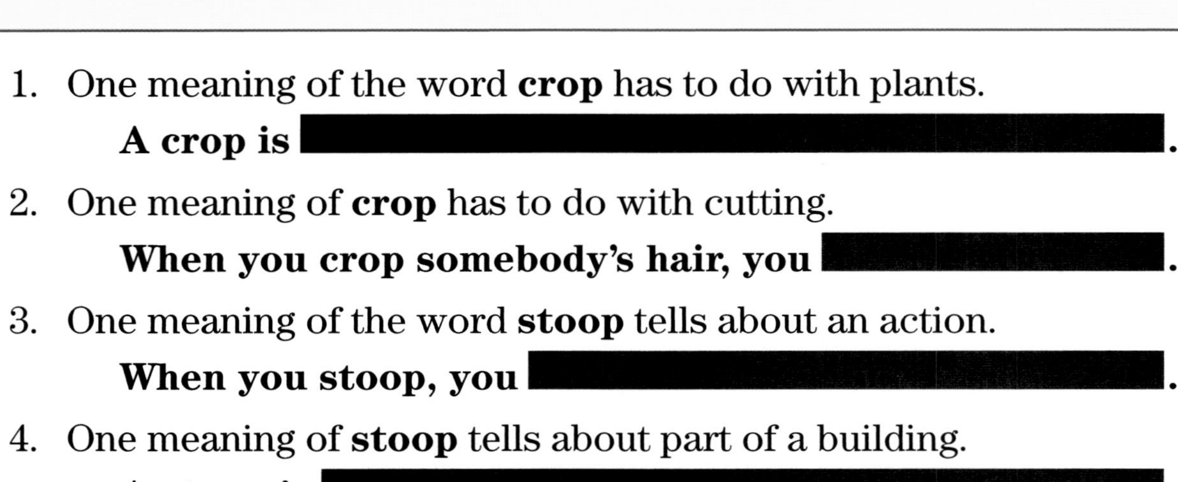

Use a dictionary to do these items.

1. One meaning of the word **crop** has to do with plants.
   A crop is ________.
2. One meaning of **crop** has to do with cutting.
   When you crop somebody's hair, you ________.
3. One meaning of the word **stoop** tells about an action.
   When you stoop, you ________.
4. One meaning of **stoop** tells about part of a building.
   A stoop is ________.

A dictionary gives you information about words. The words are listed alphabetically in the dictionary. So words that begin with the letter **A** are at the beginning of the dictionary. Words that begin with the letter **Z** are at the end of the dictionary.

A dictionary shows you how to pronounce a word. If you read a word and do not know how to pronounce it, you can look up the word in the dictionary. It has marks that show the sounds you would make to say the word. If the word has more than one syllable, the dictionary shows where each syllable begins.

A dictionary also shows word meanings. The word that you look up may have more than one meaning. For example, the word **cloud** has several different meanings. Something can **cloud** your thoughts. A **cloud** can cover the sun. The dictionary lists the meanings and tells the part of speech for each meaning. If there are synonyms for the word, the dictionary often tells about them.

The dictionary also shows special endings. If you look up the word **deer,** the dictionary will tell you that when you refer to more than one deer you don't say **deers,** you say **deer.**

1. Look up the word **woman** in the dictionary and write the spelling of the word that means **more than one woman.**
2. Look up the word **nuclear** and write the number of syllables it has.
3. Look up the word **indicate** and write the first meaning the dictionary gives.
4. Write the part of speech for the word **indicate.**

Use a dictionary to do these items.

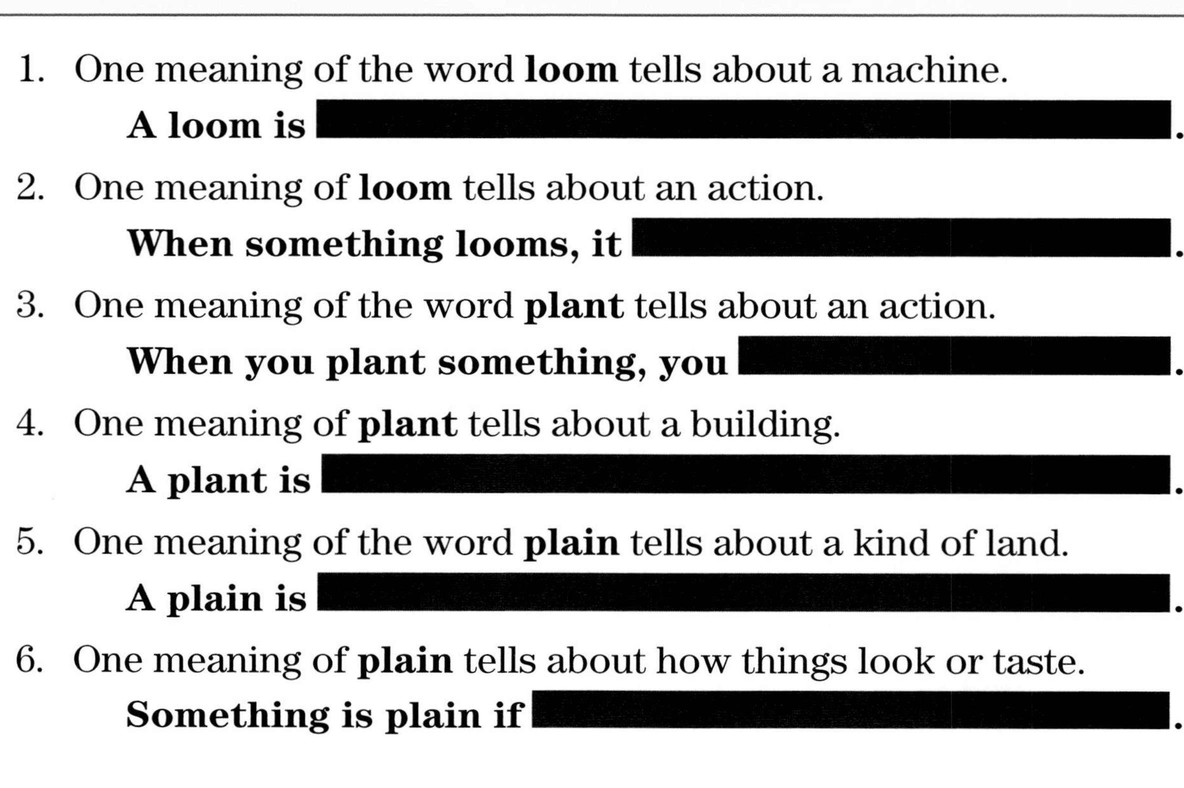

1. One meaning of the word **loom** tells about a machine.
   A loom is ________.
2. One meaning of **loom** tells about an action.
   When something looms, it ________.
3. One meaning of the word **plant** tells about an action.
   When you plant something, you ________.
4. One meaning of **plant** tells about a building.
   A plant is ________.
5. One meaning of the word **plain** tells about a kind of land.
   A plain is ________.
6. One meaning of **plain** tells about how things look or taste.
   Something is plain if ________.

For each item, write three words that alliterate with the word shown.

1. jump 2. foot 3. rusty 4. magic

An encyclopedia is a set of books that tells about any topic you could name. The topics are arranged in alphabetical order. The index of the encyclopedia is usually the last book in the set. It comes after the topics that begin with the letter **Z.** The index shows the book number and the page number for each item that is listed.

For each item, write the topic you would look up in the index of the encyclopedia.

1. What is the largest pyramid in Egypt?
2. Who was Socrates?
3. What are some of the main products of Brazil?
4. How old was Benjamin Franklin when he died?

Lesson 131

Use a dictionary to do these items.

1. One meaning of the word **pine** is about a plant.

   A pine is ________.

2. One meaning of **pine** tells how you might feel.

   When you pine, you ________.

3. One meaning of the word **story** tells about something you might hear.

   A story is ________.

4. One meaning of **story** has to do with a building.

   A story is ________.

Write a report about your favorite holiday. Use lined paper.

My Favorite Holiday

My favorite holiday is ________.

There are ________ *reasons why this is my favorite holiday.*

One reason is ________.

Another reason is ________.

One time (Tell about a personal experience.)

________.

Another time ________.

I hope ________.

For each item, write the topic you would look up in the index of the encyclopedia.

1. Why is New Orleans an important city?
2. What do reindeer eat?
3. What things did Alexander Graham Bell invent?
4. In what years was the Civil War fought?

For each item, write three words that alliterate with the word shown.

1. lightly 2. nice 3. parrot 4. buckle

Answer the questions about each simile.

- **The lake was like glass.**

1. What two things are the same?
2. How was the lake like glass?

- **Her eyes were as big as saucers.**

3. What two things are the same?
4. What's the same about her eyes and saucers?

- **Uncle Charlie moved like a bear.**

5. What two things are the same?
6. What's the same about the way Uncle Charlie and a bear moved?

- **The palm of his hand was like sandpaper.**

7. What two things are the same?
8. What's the same about his hands and sandpaper?

An atlas shows maps of different places in the world and gives information about these places. If you wanted to know how far Virginia is from Indiana, you could find that information in an atlas. If you wanted to know which states touch Illinois, you could find that information in an atlas. If you wanted to know the names of the four highest mountains in Alaska, you could find that.

An atlas has a table of contents and an index to help you find the map you're looking for.

For each item, write the topic you would look up in the atlas.

1. Which of the Great Lakes is the largest?
2. What is the capital of France?
3. What's the highest mountain in Alaska?
4. What river is on the border of Illinois?
5. What three seas touch Greece?

1. treetop   2. sandbox   3. doorknob   4. hilltop

Write the name of the part of the book you would use for each item. The answer to each item is **glossary, index,** or **table of contents.**

1. You want to find out the lesson number for the selection that starts on page 303 of your textbook.
2. You want to find out the first page number for the topic **Rocky Mountains.**
3. You want to find out the page number for the first selection in lesson 125.
4. You want to find out on what pages the topic **wheel dogs** appears.
5. You want to find out what the word **parka** means.

Write a report about your favorite subject in school.

My Favorite Subject in School

My favorite subject is (tell what) ________.

Here are three things I really like about (tell what) ________.

1. One thing I really like about ________ is ________.

2. Another thing I really like about ________ is ________.

3. Another thing I really like about ________ is ________.

Here are some of the things I have learned this year. (Tell about somethings you have learned.)

________.

Lesson 134

1. waterfall 2. rowboat 3. bookshelf 4. fireside

Write which reference book you would use to find the answer to each question. Your choices are: **dictionary, encyclopedia, atlas.**

1. How far is it from Albany, New York to Syracuse, New York?
2. Who were the rulers of England during the last 100 years?
3. What is the meaning of the word **secluded?**
4. What are the states that touch the state of Indiana?
5. In what year was Thomas Edison born?

Pretend that you're going to choose the next book the class will read. Write a paragraph that tells about the book you would choose. Tell what it is about and why you think it would be interesting to the class.

1. lighthouse
2. shoebox
3. toothbrush
4. fireball
5. lamppost

Write which reference book you would use to find the answer to each question. Your choices are: **dictionary, encyclopedia, atlas.**

1. What does the word **debunk** mean?
2. In what year was the airplane invented?
3. How many moons does the planet Uranus have?
4. How many different meanings does the word **dock** have?
5. How far is it from California to New York?

For each item, write **glossary, index** or **table of contents** to indicate the book part you would use.

1. You want to find out on how many pages the topic **husky** appears.
2. You want to find out what the word **regular** means.
3. You want to find out on what page the textbook first discusses **North Pole.**
4. You want to find out what the word **examination** means.

Write a report about the three most interesting things you learned in school this year.

The Three Most Interesting
Things I Learned

Here are the three most interesting things I learned in school this year.

1. I learned ______.

2. I learned ______.

3. I learned ______.

Here are reasons why what I learned is interesting to me.

One reason is ______ ______.

Another reason is ______ ______.